Scalable

How Financial Advisors Can Have a Great Business and a Great Life

Dan Baccarini

Copyright © 2020 Dan Baccarani
All rights reserved. No part of this book may be used or reproduced in any manner whatsoever without prior written consent of the authors, except as provided by the United States of America copyright law.

Published by Best Seller Publishing®, Pasadena, CA
Best Seller Publishing® is a registered trademark
Printed in the United States of America.
ISBN 9798591052805

This publication is designed to provide accurate and authoritative information with regard to the subject matter covered. It is sold with the understanding that the publisher is not engaged in rendering legal, accounting, or other professional advice. If legal advice or other expert assistance is required, the services of a competent professional should be sought. The opinions expressed by the authors in this book are not endorsed by Best Seller Publishing® and are the sole responsibility of the author rendering the opinion.

For more information, please write:
Best Seller Publishing®
253 N. San Gabriel Blvd, Unit B
Pasadena, CA 91107
or call 1(626) 765 9750
Visit us online at: www.BestSellerPublishing.org

Contents

Introduction 1

Chapter 1: Time: The Nonrenewable Resource 7

    Do-It-Yourself Advisors vs. Turnkey Advisors 8

    Not Enough Time to Prospect 9

    Not Enough Time to Serve Current Clients 12

    Not Enough Time to Spend with Your Loved Ones 14

Chapter 2: Riding the Roller Coaster 19

    My Business Is Controlling My Life 20

    Inconsistent and Uncertain Grown Patterns 22

    The Value of Your Practice 24

Chapter 3: Common Myths 27

    Common Misconceptions 28

    Value Propositions 28

    Delegation 30

    Planning 31

    Working Long Hours 32

    There Are No Silver Bullets 32

Chapter 4: Working on Your Business, Not in Your Business 35

Two Critical Questions: The Whats and the Hows 36
The Golden Question 38
Delegating by Checklist 39
LFD Analysis 39

Chapter 5: Outsourcing to Take Back Your Life (and Your Business) 43

The Numbers..44
Areas to Outsource...45
A Case Study 49

Chapter 6: A Systematic Approach to Creating Systems 51

Developing Systems 52
Attributes of Good Checklists 53
The Value of Checklists 56

Chapter 7: Generating Leads... 61

Reasons for Specializing 62
The Role of Specialization in Generating Leads.....................65
Sizzle and Steak..68

Chapter 8: Turning Leads into Clients 71

Turning Leads into Clients 72
The Six Phases 72
Standardizing the Process 76

Chapter 9: Turning Clients into Raging Fans 81

    The WOW Factor 83

    Customer Centricity 87

Chapter 10: Outsourcing Specifics 91

    The Importance of Outsourcing 92

    What, Specifically, Should You Outsource? 93

    A Solution for Miscellaneous Tasks 99

Conclusion 103

Bonus Chapter: Scalable Essentials 109

    Ten Essential Books for the Scalable Library 109

    Three Steps to Getting Control of Your Time 110

    The Five Reasons Someone Will Listen to You 110

    The Six Steps to Turn Prospects into Clients 111

    The Seven Topics All Prospects Must Be Educated on Before They Become Your Client 111

    The Seven Critical Areas of WOW – How to Turn Clients into Raving Fans 112

    Ten Key Traits of an Investment Management Partner 112

About the Author 115

References 117

Introduction

This book is a tale of two advisors, Johnny Do-It-Yourselfer and Sally Turnkey.

Johnny Do-It-Yourselfer has been in the business for twenty years. He has over $30 million in assets under management, which generates about $300,000 in revenue. He comes from the old school of doing things and feels he's very successful. He makes more money than anyone in his family ever has.

He's doing everything himself, including managing all his clients' assets; creating all the financial plans, when he actually has time to create a thorough plan; and conducting all of his own marketing, for which he hasn't settled on a specific system. Even after all these years, he kind of wings it quite a bit. It is more of a hope and see what works system. He networks like crazy, attending all the local networking meetings and organizations in his area, from the Rotary Club to the Chamber of Commerce to the Lions' Club. He sponsors various Little League teams to try to get his name out. He's constantly researching different investment choices for his clients, monitoring the markets for his clients, and he really doesn't have much time for social media. He considers that new school stuff. He prefers an old school approach—knocking on doors, going to meetings, and networking.

With regard to clients, Johnny sometimes slacks on returning emails and phone calls, as he really has too much on his plate, but he always gets back to his clients within a couple of days, at worst. Unfortunately, he misses a lot of family events because they're on weeknights, and weeknights are when his clients are home and available to talk. His clients have jobs, so he has to be there for them at night. That's when he has meetings with them, and that's when he talks to them on the phone. He has to do all of this after his normal work hours; he really has no choice.

At a networking event he notices a lady who turns out to be Sally Turnkey. She's also a financial advisor. Johnny has only ever seen her at this one event, but it seems as though she knows everyone really well. She's giving a hug to the head of the club and all of the other senior members. She seems to be very relaxed. She's having normal, personal, relationship conversations with people that he doesn't have. Instead, his conversations at these events tend more toward trying to see if any of the other attendees knows anyone who needs a financial advisor. It seems as though Sally is much more relaxed, and it kind of throws him for a loop. His initial thought is that she's not a huge go-getter. He suspects that she's probably not super successful in the business, but he can't help but think that she seems as though she has an air of success about her.

Johnny puts these musings in the back of his mind until the following week. He's at the meeting again, and she's also at that same networking meeting. Again, she seems very, very relaxed. He gets close to her and overhears her talking about her kids, about vacations, and different things outside of the business, and it really starts piquing his curiosity.

After the meeting, during the week, he does a bit of research on Sally. He Googles her, and checks her out on the FINRA website. Johnny finds her website and is stunned because it's so much different than his. She really doesn't talk about her business; she talks more about herself, and the relationships she's developed with clients. Sally describes the objectives she's trying to build and the goal-based planning she does with her clients.

There's nothing about investments on her website. There's nothing about specific products. All in all, it seems much more relaxed and personal than his. As he continues to research Sally, Johnny sees she's actually only been in the business for five years. This leaves him curious.

As he looks at the website, he sees that she has over $100 million under management in only five years. He raised $30 million in twenty years, and he considers himself pretty successful. He's now completely perplexed, and he has all these questions swirling in his head—mostly, he's wondering how she raised $100 million in her first five years in the business.

Thinking back to his first five years, Johnny had a phone book he was calling out of. He doesn't even know if he raised a million dollars during that time, let alone $100 million, and he's wondering how she can be so relaxed at these meetings, while he seems on edge. He's always trying to get something. He feels as though he always has a somewhat adversarial relationship with the folks at networking events.

In contrast, she seems to know everyone so well. How does she know everyone so well, and how did she build this business that seemingly is a lot different than his, but in the same field as his?

Johnny makes a decision: "That's it. Next week, if she's at the meeting, I'm going to introduce myself to her and ask her what she is doing." At the next meeting, instead of worrying about networking, he introduces himself and says, "Sally, I've been in the business for twenty years. I know you're in the same business as me. Since I'm always meeting other people in our line of work, I'm curious about your story, and how you got into the business."

Sally is as friendly as could be and says. I worked for the government for twenty years. I traveled all the time for my job. I've got two kids, and I burned out on travel. I was looking for more time at home: more time for the kids' games, more time for their practices, being home for dinner, and having more time for my spouse as well. I made the change, and I got into the financial advisory business. I was lucky to have a mentor who taught me how to do it the right way, so I could have a tremendous life and a tremendous business."

Johnny was internally stunned at this. He was thinking to himself, "How is this possible?" He has dinner at home two to three times a week, at best. Most nights, he's either meeting with clients or talking to them on the phone. Every other Saturday, he has client meetings, or is playing catch-up at the office, doing paperwork, returning calls, returning emails, or doing research. He wonders how what she's describing is possible.

Johnny says, "Listen, Sally, I've been in the business thirty years. You've only been in it five. I'm finding your story stunning. How is it possible that you've not only built a very successful advisory business, but you've also done it while not just having a life, but actually having more free time than you did before? And you did it in five years. How is that possible?"

With a grin and a twinkle in her eye, Sally says, When I first got into this business, I found the silver bullet. It's a single word that will change everything. Fortunately for me, I found it out early. Not everyone finds out what that word is. It'll change how you think, how you plan, how you build your business, how you market, how you sell, how you create plans for your client, how you do everything."

Johnny, on the edge of his seat, asks, "Well, what is that word? What is the magic bullet? Because I don't believe it exists."

Sally replies, "The answer is, 'scalable.' My business is scalable. Think about this: is everything you do scalable? If it's not, throw it out, and make it so."

"I don't get what you're talking about. I think I'm scalable. I have a successful business."

"Well, let me ask you this," she says. "Could you walk away tomorrow and have the quality of your business remain the same? Would your marketing efforts still be effective while you're on vacation? Could someone step in right now and conduct all of your new prospect meetings the same way you do? Currently, are all of your client experiences the same? Do you have a turnkey system for everything—marketing, sales, planning development, investment management, client satisfaction, annual reviews, and so on? That is what it means to be scalable, and scalability is the key to building a successful advisory business while still having a life."

Johnny sat there for a moment, feeling as though he'd been punched between the eyes because all of the things that Sally was saying that a scalable business was, were exactly what his business was not. He started to think, "What have I done wrong all these years that's allowed someone to build a business three times the size of mine, in five years, while still having a life?" This was something that Johnny thought was absolutely unfathomable.

He says, "Sally, I've been in the business a long time. I don't know if I can teach you anything, but I know you can teach me something. Would you mind sitting down with me, maybe on a weekly basis? We'll get coffee, and you can walk me through what having a scalable business means. Maybe walk me through what you did five years ago that I haven't done in the past twenty years. Let's take baby steps so that I can move from what I've considered a fairly successful business to a very successful business—a very scalable business—and still actually have a great life outside of it."

Sally enthusiastically says, "Absolutely, Johnny! Someone sat down with me five years ago and took the time with me to do this. I would have no problem doing it with you."

CHAPTER 1

Time:
The Nonrenewable Resource

At Johnny's first meeting with Sally, he has something on his mind he has been thinking about all week. He says, "Sally, I don't have enough time for everything. How can I market my business; prospect for new clients; meet with prospects; develop comprehensive financial plans for all of them; complete all their paperwork; manage all of their investments; return calls and emails in a timely manner; attend networking events; deal with compliance; meet with clients regularly; manage a staff; oversee a business that involves accounting, regulatory, banking, and HR, and still have a life? It's impossible!"

Sally says, "You're absolutely right. You cannot do all of these things. It *is* impossible. This was actually step one for me." Through Sally, I was educating myself on the nature of time, and my perspective with dealing with time. Here's what I've found:

Have you ever walked out of a meeting and said, "I'll never get that hour of my life back"? Your time is the most important resource in your financial services practice, and it is the one resource that is not renewable. You need to make sure you're using your time the right way to build and sustain your practice. Let's talk about some of the characteristics of time and what some important people have said about time.

The first thing that must be understood is that time is completely unbiased. Everybody has the same amount each day—86,400 seconds. Rich people, poor people, it doesn't matter—they all have the same amount of time. Successful people have the same amount of time as unsuccessful people do every day. That unbiased characteristic, that quality, is critical. Bill Gates has the same amount of time as I do. It doesn't matter who you are or where you come from. We all have the same amount of time and no amount of money can buy you more of it.

Peter Drucker is considered by many the most influential thinker in the history of management. He's written about countless topics. However, one of the topics that he comes back to regularly is time. He once said, "Effective people know that time is the limiting factor. Everything requires time."[1] It is the only truly universal condition—all work takes place in time and uses up time, yet most people take for granted that unique, irreplaceable, and necessary resource. Peter Drucker also said, "Nothing else perhaps distinguishes effective executives as much as their tender loving care of time."[2]

Do-It-Yourself Advisors vs. Turnkey Advisors

This book outlines the difference in approaches to business between what I'm calling the "do-it-yourself" approach and the "turnkey" approach. It leads us through a story of two different kinds of advisors—the ones who are doing things the old way, and the ones who are doing it the right, or new, way.

What are most advisors actually doing with their time, and what should most advisors be doing with it? Most advisors are bound to their businesses. In other words, their businesses are running them instead of

---

[1] Peter F. Drucker, *The Essential Drucker: The Best of Sixty Years of Peter Drucker's Essential Writings on Management*, 1st Collins Business Essentials ed. (New York, NY: Collins Business Essentials, 2008), 225.

[2] Ibid., 226.

them running their businesses. I refer to this group as do-it-yourselfers, or DIY advisors. Members of this group of advisors are trying to do everything themselves. They're not subcontracting anything out. They're outsourcing little to nothing at all.

In contrast, the other type of advisor that we're going to discuss throughout this book is the turnkey advisor. This advisor understands the importance of turnkey systems and outsourcing wherever possible. This book will tell the story of the two different types of advisors and suggest ways to transform yourself from a DIY into a turnkey advisor.

Not Enough Time to Prospect

The first main topic that I want to discuss is that advisors don't have enough time to prospect. I've been in this business since 1993, and I've spoken to thousands of other advisors during that time. They all confirm that they're only interested in two things—getting getting new clients and keeping the clients they have. That's it. Ours is a very simple business, and there are a lot of ways of doing each of those things, but those are the two key things advisors want.

Therefore, advisors need to look at how much time they are spending on those two aspects of their business as opposed to all the other aspects. When we look at not having enough time to prospect, the first bullet point is doing everything by yourself and, in turn, accomplishing little in that time. Peter Drucker, said, "I have yet to see a knowledge worker, regardless of rank or station, who could not confine something like a quarter of the demands on his time to the waste-paper basket without anybody noticing their disappearance."[3] Drucker is saying that about a fourth of what we do in a day can be thrown in the trash, and we wouldn't even notice any difference in our results. It's obvious that we

---

3 Drucker, *The Essential Drucker: The Best of Sixty Years of Peter Drucker's Essential Writings on Management*, 233.

all simply waste a lot of time. A lot of advisors are spending their time spinning their wheels on activities that don't really matter.

Two companies conducted a ten-year study analyzing over eight thousand financial advisors.[4] This was a very comprehensive study. It found that turnkey advisors spend twice as much time prospecting for new clients as opposed to do-it-yourself advisors. In other words, the do-it-yourself advisors are spending half the amount of time going after one of the most critical aspects of their business. This suggests that, if you're trying to do it yourself, and you are not scalable, you are spending half the amount of time going after new clients as opposed to the turn key advisors.

As you might expect, this results in not enough new clients. The old-school advisors, who are trying to do everything themselves, averaged four new clients a year during the course of this study, while the turnkey advisors averaged fourteen new clients a year. That's a huge discrepancy. What is amazing and interesting is that the turnkey advisors are spending twice as much time prospecting for new clients, but they're getting more than three times as many new clients. We can see that, as you spend more time prospecting, you don't get an arithmetic multiplier. Instead, you get exponential multiplication of your efforts. In other words, doubling your efforts doesn't just double your results—it can actually triple your results. The studies have proven this to be the case.

I want to emphasize the importance of thinking about time as that old, limited resource; if the number one and two top goals of your financial advisory practice are to get new clients and keep the clients you have, then look at how much time you're spending on getting new clients. That's what we're talking about here. Those who outsource, those that are scalable, those that are turnkey, spend twice as much time on this critical aspect of their businesses and experience almost triple the results.

---

4 John D. Anderson, Brad Bueermann, and Raef Lee, "A Data-Backed Solution to Building a More Profitable Advisory Business," (SEI, 2016).

The other problem with getting new clients is that many advisors have no system in place to attract them. What we find is that many people who go into business for themselves, including the advisory business, are what we call super technicians, meaning they were really good at something, and they decided to start a business in that something. They may be really good at cutting hair for a salon, but now decide, "I'm going to go start my own salon." They may be a good as a financial advisor for somebody and now step out and say, "I'm going to create my own business in the financial services arena."

The problem is a super technician does not equate to being a super businessperson. They're two different things. Running a business that specializes in something is different than specializing in something for someone else. As a result, we have a lot of good technicians that are good at getting clients, doing a great job for their clients, and good at building relationships, and so on. However, they're doing it on instinct and winging it—they're not doing it systematically. Therefore, they have no way of duplicating their results in any meaningful way in their business. In *The E Myth*, Michael Gerber refers to this as the technician's dilemma. This occurs when when someone thinks, "I'm successful at working as a financial salesperson, and as a financial planner. Therefore, I must be really good at owning a business of financial advisors." It's absolutely critical that, for effective use of time in prospecting, advisors must have a clear-cut system, step-by-step, to turn a suspect into a prospect. In other words—how do you get a normal person out there who may need financial advice to raise their hand and say, "Tell me more"?

Financial advisors absolutely need that step-by-step system. We can't just say, "Hey, I'm a nice person, so I'll just develop that relationship." Instead, we need a step-by-step system for turning you, who you raised your hand, into someone who is now my client. We've found that those advisors who don't have systems are just spinning their wheels in all different kinds of directions. They're just trying everything and searching for the silver bullet. They never find it because that sort of silver bullet doesn't exist. The actual silver bullet is in systems.

Not Enough Time to Serve Current Clients

The second aspect of a financial advisor's business that we looked at in this chapter was not having enough time to serve current clients. I said earlier that the number one priority of every financial advisor is to get more clients. Number two, and probably just as important as number one, is to keep the clients they have.

The same study of eight thousand advisors over ten years found that turnkey advisors spend 85 percent more time, or nearly double the amount of time, meeting their current clients than do-it-yourself advisors.[5] Which category of advisors do you think is going to develop a deeper relationship? If I'm spending ten hours a week on meeting my existing clients, and the turnkey advisor is spending eighteen and a half hours or almost double, that advisor is probably going to develop a deeper relationship with existing clients. That's important for the next step, which is referrals.

If you do not have a deep relationship with a service provider, you're not going to give them referrals. It's a matter of fact. One study shows that if you have high trust in your financial advisor, you're 94 percent likely to give referral. If you have low trust, you are 70 percent likely to NOT give a referral, and more likely to switch your advisor.[6] Accordingly, the trust that comes with a deepened relationship is absolutely a critical component as to generating the client satisfaction that's going to lead

---

5   Anderson, Bueermann, and Lee, "A Data-Backed Solution to Building a More Profitable Advisory Business."

6   CEG_Worldwide, "Investor Dashboard: An in-Depth Look at Investor Behavior Trends," (Vanguard, 2018), 13.

someone into becoming a raving fan. You can't do that by spending half as much time as your competitors on developing relationships.

The next key point is that DIY advisors are vulnerable to competitors. A study by Spectrem Research[7] looked at the top five reasons clients may switch advisors. Advisors assume that the number one reason would be that an advisor's performance was bad, putting the client in bad investments.

No. In fact, the number one reason a client may switch advisors is for not returning phone calls in a timely manner. The third reason is not being proactive in contacting clients, and number four is not returning emails in a timely manner. That means that three of the top five reasons that a client is going to fire you, their advisor, all have to do with time. If you're trying to do everything yourself, how are you going to have enough time to return calls and emails in timely manner?

The Spectrem study goes on to define "timely" because timely could mean something different to me than it does to you. The study found that 22 percent of affluent respondents, about one out of four people, want a return call within two hours,[8] and more than a third want emails returned within two hours. We're not merely saying that they want a response the same day; they want a reply within two hours. That's a very short window. Just imagine that you're spending all your time doing other things in your business, such as paperwork, marketing, research, trading, social media, and so on because you're a do-it-yourselfer. However, the turnkey advisor has outsourced all of these ancillary tasks and can instead focus, on client service. In other words, once you've outsourced everything except client service, you've got a scalable business. You now have the time to follow up with clients in a timely manner.

Remember, if you don't call within two hours, one out of four clients is not happy AND that's the number one reason they will fire you.

---

[7] Spectrem_Group, "The Affluent Investor: Insights and Opportunities for Advisors," (2016), 30.

[8] Ibid., 31.

That's really important stuff. Here's another interesting fact: 43 percent of clients don't want a return call from anyone else but you.[9] They don't want your assistant to call, they don't want a partner to call, they don't want a scheduler to call, and they don't want your office administrator to call. They want you to call.

We're going to talk throughout this whole book about things that you can outsource. We're also going to talk about some things you can't outsource. This is one of them. Obviously, if you're a do-it-yourselfer, and you're not outsourcing, there is no way you're ever going to be able to satisfy your clients' timely communication needs. That's unfortunate if one of your major objectives is keeping the clients you have, as this is the top reason that clients fire their advisors—you don't want to be one of those advisors who gets fired for such an easily fixable issue.

Not Enough Time to Spend with Your Loved Ones

The final piece of making your time inside your financial advisory business count is that most advisors don't have enough time to have a life outside their practice. The average advisor works over fifty hours a week. Most also work weeknights, and they average about six hours or so during the weekend. It makes sense that most advisors put in time at night to provide better service for their clients. Because most clients are at work during the day, most advisors have to meet their clients at night, but maybe you'd prefer to spend time with your family and friends on nights and weekends.

Obviously, if you're trying to do everything yourself, and you don't have a scalable business, you're going to spend more time not meeting with your clients because you're personally doing all the other tasks of running the business—all the administrative research and technology aspects of the business.

---

9   Ibid.

I used to be a financial advisor myself, so I understand. Most advisors find that they are not running their businesses anymore. Instead, their businesses are running them. The important thing is that I'm trying to let you know that you can have a successful business if you do the right things with your time. If you don't, you're NOT only not going to have a great business, you're also NOT going to have a great life. I want you to have both of those things. It is important to note that with a scalable business or practice, you'll be able to achieve both goals.

Obviously, if you're the only person who's handling everything in your business, you're never going to be able to unplug. If you're all by yourself, how are you going to go on vacation? What happens if, all of a sudden, you have a health or personal issue? If something gets messed up on an account, you've got to deal with it, if you are letting the business run you, instead of you running your business. One of the things that we're going to talk about throughout this book is working on your business instead of working in your business.

I want to reference Peter Drucker again. He says that effective executives do not start out with planning; they start by finding where their time actually goes.[10] Consequently, we're going to talk about analyzing your time. Step one is tracking your time in real time. Do this in fifteen-minute increments for a week. Track it all, whether you're going to the restroom, if you're taking a coffee break, if you're making a phone call, if you're talking to your spouse, or if you're checking Facebook. For fifteen minutes, be honest with yourself. Analyze one week in fifteen-minute increments on a sheet of paper or a day planner to keep it organized. Drucker recommends doing this for three or four weeks. I think one should suffice. However, it's got to be a very honest accounting of your time.

---

10 Drucker, *The Essential Drucker: The Best of Sixty Years of Peter Drucker's Essential Writings on Management*, 233.

Step two is to look back and determine your time wasters. What is the 25 percent that you can throw in the trash can that's not going to make any difference? How much time are you spending with your existing clients? How much time are you spending getting new clients? Look not only at what you can throw out, but also what can you outsource. What can somebody else do for you at a low cost that can come off of your plate?

The final piece, step three, is the planning part. You have to block your time. Allocate it in blocks of focused activities. I don't start making prospecting calls, go and check emails, return a client's call, then take a call from a vendor. No. I block out one to two hours of only prospecting calls. I don't return any calls at that time. I don't schedule anything else during that time. I don't check my emails during that time. I don't look at Facebook during that time. I don't check the news during that time. I don't check the markets during that time. All I do for two hours is prospect. All I do for one hour is call existing clients. Whatever it is, you've got to block your time and schedule these focused activities.

Remember: you cannot get any more time. This is all you have. How are you going to spend it?

After Sally imparts this knowledge during their meeting, Johnny says, Sally, "I get it now. It all begins with the realization that time is a nonrenewable resource. We all have the same amount of time that we can use; the difference between successful people and unsuccessful people is what do we do with this resource? Step one: I need to track all my time usage. What am I doing with my time? Step two is to analyze it. Am I doing the right things at the right time? Am I wasting time in any areas? Step three is to plan the usage of my time in blocks.

"One of my big problems," he continues, "is that I'll start one thing. Then I'll get distracted with an email. Then I'll have to take a phone call. Then I'll go back to something else. Before I know it, the day's gone, and I didn't accomplish what I wanted to. Instead, I need to block out my time for specific tasks—maybe one hour for just prospecting, one hour for Facebook marketing, one hour for research—so I have all my time specifically blocked out, and I ignore everything else during that timeframe."

Sally says, "That's exactly what you need to do. Do that for a couple of weeks, and let me know how it goes."

CHAPTER 2:

Riding the Roller Coaster

Sally asks Johnny, "So, how did it go the past couple of weeks as you analyzed your time usage?"

Johnny replies, "It was difficult to do, but so worth it. I was able to see when I was actually using my time profitably. Even better, that exercise helped me find the time wasters. I think I discovered a good method for how to block my time out, although the blocks still need a little tweaking."

"However, I'm still having some difficulty with a few other things," he adds. "What I find is that I'm really good, maybe even way above, average as an advisor, but not at running my business. I'm probably average at best running my business. The judges might score me a 9 or a 10 as an advisor, but I'm only a 3 or 4 as a business owner. Instead of running my business, what I find is my business is now running my life."

"Has this ever happened to you?" he asks. "I feel like I'm on a roller coaster. I'll have great months mixed in with bad months. My income's great this month, and then the next month it's not, or this quarter's great, but the next quarter's horrible. I don't know if it's just part of my business or whether it's due to some external reason. I find that I am the business. Without me, there is nothing. So, do I really have a business, or am I just an overworked employee with nothing of value to show?"

Sally says, " Johnny, you're really insightful on this. I told you once you change your view of time, it's going to awaken you to what a real business is, and more importantly, what a real business is not. Ready for lesson two?"

This chapter, Riding the Roller Coaster, describes the two main problems that DIY advisors have; the first is that the business is controlling their lives, and the second is that the business exhibits inconsistent and uncertain growth patterns. Let's examine each problem in turn.

My Business Is Controlling My Life

Do-it-yourselfers are stuck in the technician's dilemma, as described by Michael Gerber in his book *The E Myth*.[11] The technician's dilemma occurs when you're really good at something, but that does not mean you're really good at running the business of something. For example, your barber may be a really good barber, but that doesn't mean he's good at running a barber shop. It's the same with financial advisors. They may be, very good at being a financial advisor, but it doesn't necessarily mean they're great at running a business.

What happens is that these financial advisors end up trying to do everything, because they're not good at delegating—they always feel that if it's going to get done right, they have to be the one getting it done. They get stuck in being the technician of everything, instead of being the entrepreneur of their business. They end up having a mindset of "without me, nothing can get done properly." There are financial advisors who are answering the phones, returning all the calls, producing all the plans, scheduling all the meetings, doing all the prospecting, and creating all of the Facebook posts. They are doing it all themselves, or at least trying to do it all themselves, and quite frankly, not getting it done efficiently or effectively. Even worse, they're spending too much money in all the wrong places, because they're the most expensive employee probably in

---
11 Gerber, *The E-Myth: Why Most Businesses Don't Work and What to Do About It*.

their firm, if they have other employees. Their business is controlling their life, and they have the mindset of "without me, it's not going to grow" which is a really, really big problem. It is because of this mindset that is keeping the business from growing. That mindset is what is going to prevent them from scaling their business.

The other aspect of this challenge is that these advisors are also involved in every aspect of the business; they're not outsourcing, and they're not delegating because they are fearful of giving up control. They're fearful of having someone else do something. They are reviewing every email going out. They're involved in every aspect of the business. The result of that is that they're then tethered to the business. The business becomes a ball and chain. It becomes a burden instead of an opportunity. What you find is that among the vast majority of financial advisors, their business cannot exist without their involvement because they're everything. What they think was going to be freedom has now become a prison.

A lot of advisors have this issue. They wanted to start a business for themselves because they wanted to create freedom for themselves. They didn't want to be tethered to their job or employer, but now they're tethered to their business, and it's even a worse prison because it's all up to them. This business is now controlling their life, thus creating their ball and chain. Every single problem of the business now becomes the advisor's problem.

Not only are these advisors tethered to the business, but it also gets worse—just think about the emotional drain that happens to do-it-yourself advisors with every phone call that's negative, every problem with the business, and every little error. Many advisors have 100, 200, or even 300 clients. Let's say that 10 percent of clients have an issue every few months. That still means that twenty to thirty of their clients will have issues every couple of months. If the advisor is the only one solving the problems, then those twenty to thirty problems are going to just keep piling up and piling up and piling up on their shoulders. Think of the image of Atlas with the world on his shoulders—it evokes all of these problems piling up on the advisors' shoulders. There is simply no one else that DIY advisors "trust" to help solve all these problems. I have seen the emotional drain and the emotional burnout many times among the financial advisors I have worked with.

During my travels, I have personally met with hundreds of advisors. I've seen the emotional drain with my own eyes, where they are thinking, "I just need to get out of this business." This stands in huge contrast to the people who know how to delegate and who are in a scalable business. Members of the group of advisors that I'm calling "turnkey advisors" are enjoying their life and enjoying their business. There is a stark contrast between the two.

Inconsistent and Uncertain Grown Patterns

The second thing that occurs when DIY advisors rely solely on themselves is that they end up creating an inconsistent practice. They end up riding a roller coaster with a business that has a great month, then a bad month, a great quarter, then a bad quarter, and a great year before a bad year. They don't have a repeatable, sustainable business. Instead, they have a business that's based on their individual efforts.

The sales-and-business funnel becomes very inconsistent. They will do a lot of prospecting work to get a batch of new leads, then they spend all their time in shepherding those names, those leads, those prospects through to becoming a client. They then wake up two months later and realize they don't have any new prospects, so they start back at the beginning thinking, "I need to get more prospects," shepherd them through the funnel, and continually experience this roller coaster of inconsistent results.

Miller Heiman, in a book called *The New Strategic Selling*,[12] described this roller coaster effect. It is all the result of advisors not having enough time to focus on all aspects of the sales cycle, or the client development cycle, because they have only enough time to focus on one aspect of the funnel, instead of doing it the right way, where they're focusing on almost all the pieces at the same time. Focusing on the big picture will eliminate this roller coaster effect. As DIY investors don't delegate, it is virtually impossible for them to have a smooth, repeatable, sustainable business that is consistent because they just don't have the time to actually work on the front end of the client development funnel, the back end of the client development funnel, and everything in between. They just can't do it—there's not enough time available each and every day.

Every successful advisor that I've seen has a team and a process to work their clients, prospects, and leads through this funnel, while still putting new names into the front end of the funnel. They have the time to put them in the front end, work the middle, and close them in the back end. There is a systematic way in which to turn your prospects into clients. This is discussed in detail in a later chapter.

The third thing that results from this DIY approach is that riding the roller coaster makes future forecasting a completely wild guess. It's very difficult for DIY advisors to forecast accurately when they're running the business themselves or doing it with very limited resources. Forecasting is near-impossible because they don't know the answers to variables such as: *What if I get sick? What if I need to come out of the business for a little bit? Will I ever be able to take a real vacation? What if I need to care for a loved one? Who knows what will happen to my practice and my business?* If I'm running my practice by myself, it's like having a factory with one machine. It's risky because if anything happens to that one

---

12 Stephen E. Heiman, Diane Sanchez, and Tad Tuleja, *The New Strategic Selling: The Unique Sales System Proven Successful by the World's Best Companies*, Warner Books ed. (New York, NY: Warner Books, 1998).

machine, all of my planning goes out the window. It's very, very difficult for me to be able to build a business that's sustainable, repeatable, and consistent if it's just me. How can I plan for the future? Everything I do is basically just a number I'm scratching on the paper versus actually coming up with something that's real, based upon running an actual system.

The Value of Your Practice

All of this uncertainty and consistency flows down to valuation. How valuable is your advisory business or your financial planning practice, if you're basically the center of everything? One article from *Wealth Management*, called "What is Your Advisory Practice Really Worth?", says that practices with owner-centric branding have unattractive revenue streams. The more the owner is central to the business, the more unattractive that revenue stream is to a potential buyer, which means a lower valuation. The article goes on to say, "If an advisor is the primary relationship manager with the clients in the firm, then the risk to the buyer is greater." Their solution is be sure the clients all have multiple touch points within the firm beyond the primary advisor. The bottom line is that if the owner is the primary driver of the business, the valuation of that business is going to be lower.[13]

Another article out of *FA Magazine* called "The True Value of Your Practice" says, "The ability for someone new to take over a business with minimal disruption goes hand in hand with that business's sustainability and ultimately its value."[14] They want to know to what extent the business is transferable and sustainable. If I'm doing everything myself, then want to sell the business, that business isn't very transferable because the business is just me. Thus, I must create a business that's sustainable

---

13 John Furey and Matt Cooper, "What Is Your Advisory Practice Really Worth?," *Wealth-Management Magazine*2013.
14 Matt Matrisian, "The True Value of Your Practice," *FA Magazine*, March 2, 2015 2015.

and isn't centered around one person or even a couple of people. I've got to center it around the business and around clear systems.

And if the name of the business is Dan and Associates, and I want to sell it to Alex, that's not really good, right? All my clients know the business as Dan and Associates. But now Alex wants to come in, and Dan is going away. This example illuminates what an owner-centric business is and what it should not be. One very simple tip is just on the generic naming of companies. You might consider something like Newport or West Coast Advisors. It doesn't matter, but you want a generic name because you're hoping to become less owner centered.

This is just one example of what advisors need to be thinking about when they're creating a scalable business. They don't want to make it owner-centric. They have to get out of every detail of the business. They need to think about how their business will be transferrable. If I stepped away for six months, does the business still run? That should be in the thought process of every single advisor out there.

Johnny tells Sally, "Now I understand the technician's dilemma. It's starting to make sense why my income was on a rollercoaster. I have to learn how to prioritize my time with my sales funnel and with my business prospects. Most importantly, I completely understand that the value of my business is much lower if it's just me. There's really no business to buy. If it's all on my shoulders, if the business is just Johnny, there's not much value for someone to purchase it from me in case I ever want to retire and sell my business. I need to actually create a business that's beyond myself; and that is something I'm just now learning, and it's difficult because I have been stuck in that technician's dilemma forever."

Sally says, "That was a hard part for me to get dialed in, too. It takes a little practice. But the good news is that I'm here to help. You don't have to do it alone."

Exercise for the Reader:

The following exercises should help you get a clearer picture of the sustainability of your business:

- Review your sales and revenue from month to month. How consistent have you been? Do you have dry spells? Would you like to solve this issue?
- If you stepped away from your business for one, two, three, four, five, or six months, what would happen? An advisor needs to examine every aspect of their business as to what happens if they're gone. If it looks like it's going to fail, then you've got a problem. You don't have a scalable business; instead, you have a prison.

CHAPTER 3:

Common Myths

As Johnny and Sally sit back down for another one of their visits, Sally notices that Johnny's demeanor has changed. He's not that excited. He seems rather sullen, in fact, so she asks him what's wrong. Johnny says, "As I think about this more, I don't know if this scalable, outsourcing stuff will work for me."

Sally says, "Talk to me. Tell me what you're thinking. What's your problem?"

Johnny says, "I think three things are issues. The first is my value proposition. My value proposition for my client is that I'm the one that's doing everything. I'm their go-to. I'm the one that's managing their portfolios. I'm the one that's selecting everything. I'm the one that is taking care of them. I'm the one that's doing everything. If, all of a sudden, I wasn't the one doing everything, what's my value proposition? I don't know if my client would be willing to pay for me to just outsource everything to someone else.

Number two is delegation. I'm not good at delegating. When I delegate, the work product seems to reduce. The quality of work is not to my standards when I delegate, and I'm fearful that if I start having other people do stuff, then it's not going to get done right.

The third thing may just come from an old school belief that I need to work long hours. I'm a believer that the more you work, the more you make. With all of that combined, this week I've run into a mental roadblock."

Sally says, "Everything you're saying is BS. I'm just telling it to you straight. That's why I'm here; I'm not here to make you feel good, because that's not going to help you get the results you want. This is what we call head trash. You are always limited by your own head trash. These beliefs are what we call broken records. The myths that you're holding onto are going to prevent you from taking a step forward. It's not at all uncommon. You may think, 'Oh my practice is different,' but I'm going to tell you that your practice isn't different. The beliefs that you just described for me are not different. A lot of advisors have the same head trash, and it's absolutely key to address all of those false beliefs. While you brought up three things, there are actually five common myths when it comes to building a scalable business."

Common Misconceptions

Many financial advisors I've talked to hold misconceptions about the best way to run their businesses. This chapter will attempt to dispel some of these myths.

Value Propositions

Common myth number one is, "My value proposition is that I'm the money manager creating a specific allocation and model portfolios for my clients." In other words, what many financial advisors are saying is, "I can't outsource. I've got to do it all myself. I've got to be a do-it-yourselfer versus an outsourcer because that's the value that I'm bringing to my clients. If I'm giving that to somebody else, then there's no value that I'm bringing to the relationship with my client."

Fortunately, this belief is becoming less and less prevalent. Not that long ago, more than half of financial advisors thought this way. Now less than half of advisors think this, but we're still talking 40%, roughly.[15] The good news is that clients don't believe it.

The Investor Dashboard, a survey of thousands of financial services clients, asked, "What are the things that you rank highly in a financial advisor?" The number one response was someone who provides transparency in their interactions. The number two response was someone who provides prompt follow-up on requests. And number three was someone who takes the time to understand needs, goals, and risk tolerances.[16] In other words, the top three reasons have nothing to do with the idea that a financial advisor is doing it all themselves. "My financial advisor's picking every single one of my investments, creating my portfolio, running the money, and making my trades" is not in the top three. Clients don't care about that stuff. As a result, it's extremely important that advisors understand that being a do-it-yourselfer does not represent their value proposition. That is not what the clients rank as extremely important with a financial advisor.

In that same study, the primary reasons behind client satisfaction came down to reputation/trust and this finding was consistent across Millennials, Gen-Xers, and Baby Boomers. Number one is reputation or trust. Numbers two and three are relationship and service. Advice came in fourth. Investment performance is fifth. But what should be interesting to note is that clients are not putting value on the do-it-yourselfer. Nowhere in this report is it saying, "I value this relationship because the advisor's doing everything themselves." Clients value their relationship for transparency, for service, for advice, and for understanding their needs. The notion or myth of, "My value proposition is that I'm doing it all myself," is completely false. It's purely what we refer to as a broken record in the advisor's head.

---

15 Anderson, Bueermann, and Lee, "A Data-Backed Solution to Building a More Profitable Advisory Business."
16 CEG_Worldwide, "Investor Dashboard: An in-Depth Look at Investor Behavior Trends," 9.

Delegation

The second myth this chapter aims to debunk is: "Delegating is going to reduce the effectiveness of my office." This could also be said as: "Hiring folks is going to reduce the effectiveness because I can do it better," or "I am the only one that can perform a particular task the right way."

This misconception has its roots in two thought patterns. One is the trap that by being very good technicians in something we then have the tendency to feel that then we're good at everything, which is false. I may be very good at cutting hair, but that doesn't mean I'm good at doing the books for my business. The smart barbershop owner decides to outsource this. It's the same with a financial services business. I may be very good at getting new clients or good at providing advice, but that doesn't mean I'm good at handling my social media, running my office, setting my appointments, or managing the money.

The consulting firm McKinsey estimates the benefits of outsourcing are worth three to ten times the cost. If I spend $1,000 a week or a month on outsourcing, I'm going to reap benefits of between $3,000 and $10,000. The value of outsourcing is undisputable. A report called "A Data-Backed Solution to Building a More Profitable Advisory Business," by CEG Worldwide, a leading consulting firm for the financial advisory business, states that, "Just because you can do something does not mean that you should do it."[17]

Advisors, or entrepreneurs in general, think, "Well, I can do that. So, I should do it." No. You have more valuable things to do. In fact, you should zealously guard your time and use it as effectively as possible.

The idea that delegating is harmful is rooted in a second misconception—financial advisors commonly think they need to hire a big staff if they're going to ramp up growth. People get spooked when

---

[17] Anderson, Bueermann, and Lee, "A Data-Backed Solution to Building a More Profitable Advisory Business," 6.

they think the only way that they can scale their business is by hiring a lot of people. Nowadays, this is the biggest myth out there.

I owned a consulting firm for the financial services industry that, at one point, had twenty total employees. With the advent of email technology and social networking sites, we now have one employee, and we do more business than ever. By leveraging technology and outsourcing, we don't need to hire a huge staff. Most financial advisory practices will have a staff, but they need to make sure it's twenty-first century staff, not twentieth century staff. By twentieth century staff, I mean that every menial task was done by the staff. In contrast, twenty-first century staffers now understand that most menial tasks can be done with technology. In the twentieth century, yes, to be scalable, you did have to have a big staff. In the twenty-first century, this is no longer the case.

Planning

Many advisors think, "I do not have the time to plan my business. I'm too busy working in my business." That same study, *A Data-Backed Solution to Building a More Profitable Advisory Business,* states that 67 percent of survey respondents agree or somewhat agree that not having enough time to focus on growing their business is a significant pain point. So, this is, again, the entrepreneurial trap where we let the business run our lives instead of us running our business. We've got it flip-flopped.

So many advisors and entrepreneurs feel that they don't have enough time to plan their business because they're working in their business, not working on their business. I recommend that they set aside a specific amount of time, either on a weekly basis or a monthly basis to get away from the office and plan. Don't go to the office. Take half a day and go somewhere else. Go to the local library (yep, they still exist and they are even quieter than ever) to spend some time simply thinking about your business, away from email, away from phones, and away from distractions, so that you can actually work on your business. This is absolutely critical. Then, on an annual basis, there should be some sort of several-day planning session where you, your partners, and/or your staff are getting away to specifically plan on your business and work on your business, rather than constantly working in your business. Working on your business is what's going to grow your business; Working in your business is not going to grow your business. It's just going to maintain your business.

Working Long Hours

Many financial advisors, and businesspeople in general, believe that working long hours and working hard will eventually mean success. This is a huge myth in every industry and within all walks of life. In reality, working hard and efficiently are what lead to success. It has nothing to do with the time you spend working in the business. Instead, how efficiently are you using that time? I could work twenty hours a day, but if I'm not working efficiently, then I'm not going to grow my business. It's all about working smarter, working more efficiently, and leveraging your time and resources to increase your effectiveness and increase your results. That is what's going to grow your business, not spending more hours in the business. That is not the formula at all. Efficiency and effectiveness are the things that matter, not the length of time that you're doing something.

There Are No Silver Bullets

Other advisors believe, "There's a silver bullet to this business that, once I find it, all of my issues will be solved." Have you heard business owners making statements such as, "Once I get the next seminar created, once I get the new website created, once I figure out the new investment product I'm going to use, once I implement the new marketing method"?

Unfortunately, there is no silver bullet. If there was, someone would be marketing that silver bullet, and it would actually be completely replicable to everybody else. But it does not exist.

Actually, the silver bullet is finding what works for you, finding the right market, and working that market efficiently. Now, there are other intricacies that go into this, but there is no shortcut to success. It takes a lot of effort in taking the right, effective steps to create your success. There is no silver bullet. We don't just buy this, subscribe to that, or create this, which all lead to this incredible business. It's all about doing the right things with the right people enough times. That is the formula to create success. One variation on the silver-bullet misconception is, "If I build a better mouse trap, I'm sure to succeed." In other words, people think, "I've got the best model in the world, the greatest investment plan that exists," but no one's going to just flock to you. You still have to market it. Our industry is littered with great ideas that failed because they were never executed. I always say I would rather have a poorly written plan executed well than a well-written plan executed poorly.

You've got to have the execution. You've got to take action. A lot of entrepreneurs, a lot of advisors, sit back and want to create something that will generate action. Instead, they are the ones must generate the action.

On the flip side, I have seen a tremendous number of successful advisors who weren't that great; They didn't even have good ideas. They weren't super sharp, but you know what? They took action. They had effective activities. They talked to the right people, saying the right things enough times to be successful. A lot of people focus on saying the right thing or creating the right thing, but they don't talk to the right people, and they definitely don't do it enough times. They all are about the creation of the right idea, the better mouse trap. They're not about the other part of the equation, talking to the right people enough times.

These misconceptions are the most common that I have encountered in my career when talking to thousands of financial advisors over the past quarter century. Others ones are out there, but these are the ones I see the most often leading to business plateaus or roadblocks.

As Johnny listens to Sally, he sees himself in her words. He tells her, "I get it. I understand that if I hold onto these beliefs, I cannot go forward. Even in my personal life, I'm sure I have head trash in other areas."

Sally says, "You're absolutely right. Head trash is most often used as excuses not to change. I'm no different. Most of it is simply your internal voice talking you out of making changes. There's a saying that doing the same thing and expecting different results is the definition of insanity. You can't do the same things over and over and over again and expect different results; that is insane. You must change what you're doing. And more often than not, changing what you're doing begins with changing what you're thinking."

Exercise for the Reader:

Now is the time. Break away for two to three hours to plan and work on your business. Even if you have no time at the moment, then just take fifteen minutes to do this. What are the things that are holding you back from creating a scalable business? Write them down. Are they any of the ones that we've just talked about, or is there something else? Write down what it is about the obstacles that you see as limiting your ability to build a scalable business. How can you overcome these hurdles?

CHAPTER 4

Working on Your Business, Not in Your Business

When Johnny and Sally next meet, he says, "Since we talked last week, I've worked hard to clear my mind of all the head trash. I know some of it's still there, but I feel ready to take the next step. Where should I begin? What should I do next?"

Sally says, "It's actually pretty simple. You need to spend time working on your business instead of in your business."

"That sounds easy enough," Johnny says, "but it is something I always have difficulty with."

Sally replies, "It does sound easy, but actually it's not. Remember when we talked about the technician's dilemma? The technician's dilemma, if you don't recall, is a situation where having one job skill doesn't necessarily translate to running a business based around performing that skill. Let's say you're really good at something; in this case, you're good at being a financial adviser. However, that does not necessarily mean that you're good at building a successful financial advisory business. Therefore, you spend time in your business instead of on your business. That's why you're having issues. It's because you're a really good technician.

The first time that we sat down, we talked about time. And studies have shown that successful financial advisors spend more time working on their business, as opposed to be a prisoner in their business.

"It's somewhat of a confusing thought, Johnny. "If you spend more time on your business, eventually you're going to spend less time working in and on your business than if you just focused on working in your business. In the end, working on your business is going to save you time. This is the key to building a scalable business."

This chapter probably represents the most overlooked change you can make in your business. It's such an amorphous thing to say: "Work on your business, not in your business." What does that really mean? How often should someone do this? What, specifically, should they be doing?

This leads us right back to the entrepreneurial trap, which tells us that we're always performing the intricacies of the business. As a financial planner, I spend all my time planning, meeting with clients, marketing my business, making phone calls, researching investments, and doing paperwork. That's all the stuff that my business requires, but that's not what we should be doing or how we build our business.

Two Critical Questions: The Whats and the Hows

Working on your business is looking at more of the hows than the whats. We don't spend enough time on answering two critical questions: what is my business actually doing, and how are we doing all of these things? Here's an important point—financial advisory is not what my business does.

Some people might say, "I am a financial advisor, that's what my business does." No, it's not. What my business does are all the little bits and pieces that make up my financial advisory practice. When I look at what my business is actually doing, I need to look at all of those intermediary steps to get to the end goal of my business.

The end goal of my business is a financial advisory practice. It's kind of like a factory. When we look at a factory or a manufacturing company, the end goal is to make a car, but that's not what we do—we don't just put raw materials in, and a car comes out. We have hundreds, if not thousands, of intermediary steps that we take to actually build a car. So, what a factory actually does is all those little things that lead to the end goal of making a car. If we're going to improve or work on a business of building cars, we don't look at what the end goal is; We must look at all of the intermediary steps. How can we get better at those specific intermediary steps?

The problem with the financial advisory business is that we don't analyze our business in that respect. We say, "I want to get twenty new clients." We need to think what are all the specific steps we need to take to get those clients? What are all the intermediary steps? That's the part that we look at when we are looking at working on our business, not in our business. When we're working in our business, we're actually doing all of the intermediary steps, but when we're working on our business, we're analyzing those intermediary steps.

Most advisors look at their business and all the intermediary steps only when they're having a problem. Let's say, as an example, they are not getting enough clients, but want more. So, they now ask, "Okay, what are all the steps I need to take to get new clients?" If they are having issues with operations, they ask, "Okay, what are all the steps that we're doing in operations that are leading to our mistakes, so we can correct them?"

The only time most advisors and entrepreneurs actually work on their business is when they have a problem in a specific area, and then they don't work on their business holistically. They work on it with a very myopic vision—only on those specific areas that they're trying to fix, instead of having a holistic vision of their entire business. This is a big issue that we have as entrepreneurs in general.

An advisor needs to take himeself out of being an advisor, which seems weird. They're in the advisory business, but when they work on the business, they need to think of it more as a CEO. This means that they need to look at everything in a very broad aspect. This is a habit that advisors must get into—continuously looking at their business as the CEO would-not as the guy who is executing all the stuff within their business. This is a critical habit that every successful advisor must develop.

The Golden Question

What, specifically, should they be thinking about? I call this the golden question, which is simply this: what can I systematize in my business? We need to look at every area of our business and design every step whether it's getting clients, keeping clients, obtaining referrals, financial planning, planning analysis, paperwork, or anything else. What can we systematize? How can we create a system for every single aspect of our business? This is the most important question that advisors can ask themselves on an ongoing basis. This is the key to building a scalable business.

What areas can you systematize? Think checklists. In a later chapter, we're going to go in depth on how to create systems, and we're going to talk about checklists specifically. However, for now, ask yourself, "What is the system for every piece of my business?"

As you can see, working on your business is a pretty big task. That's why I say the most important thing that a scalable advisor can do for their business is work on their business. You need to figure out what systems can be created within the business and what can be systematized.

Checklists are foundations of systems. Take a look at a book called *The Checklist Manifesto*,[18] which I think is fantastic. As you think about

---

18 Atul Gawande, *The Checklist Manifesto: How to Get Things Right*, 1st ed. (New York, NY: Metropolitan Books, 2010).

systematizing your business, you need to be thinking in checklists. How can you create checklists to run the specific areas of business that you are systematizing?

Delegating by Checklist

The other question that needs to be asked is: What tasks can others do, as opposed to me doing these tasks? This is another of those critical areas that is difficult for advisors to do. When they create all of their systems, and they create all the different checklists, pieces, and intermediary steps, they need to highlight what those areas are that somebody else can do, so that you, specifically, do not need to do yourself.

Many advisors are trying to do everything in their practice. Just because you can do it doesn't mean you should do it. You need to look at all those tasks that only you can do, and those tasks that you can delegate to others. This is a very important area for building a scalable business and breaking out of the entrepreneur trap.

LFD Analysis

The other area that you should be looking at is what I call the LFD analysis. The LFD analysis is simply the lowest financial denominator. When we look at all the different intermediary steps for creating a scalable business for all the systems, we need to look at what the lowest financial denominator of each of these steps is. In other words in what areas can I get someone or something else to do this for me cheaper than I can do it myself?

I'm the highest financial denominator in my business, typically; I'm an elite financial advisor. If I have a second-in-command, another high-to-medium paid wage-earner in my practice, that person may not be the right person to do all of the menial paperwork. I shouldn't be doing it, either. Is there somebody else that I can use as the lowest financial denominator for that specific task?

As we start analyzing and working on our business, we need to be cognizant of the lowest financial denominator for each of these specific tasks. Can I outsource it? Can I use technology? The technology solution could be more expensive than the solution I have within my office because some technology is very expensive. However, menial tasks can be outsourced for a much lower financial denominator than most advisors are currently spending.

The lowest financial denominator is absolutely a key to growing your business in a scalable and economically responsible manner. We can all scale our businesses if we just hire a bunch of people or spend a bunch of money on technology, but the key to not doing that is the LFD, the lowest financial denominator. This analysis is going to allow us to build a scalable business and do it in an economically responsible manner.

Johnny says, "I can really see how working *on* your business is critical to building a scalable business. I really have a lot to think about, especially the golden question. What can I systematize in my business? Additionally, I never thought about the lowest financial denominator before. I never applied that logic to my business. My plan is to look for the LFD that I can apply to different areas within my business because I'm the highest financial denominator in my company. So, if I'm doing a task, it needs to be a very high-value task, as opposed to using my high-value financial dominator on a low-value task. I need to align where I'm spending my time, other people's time, expensive time, and less expensive time. That is an analysis that I never thought of before in my business."

Sally says, "Its great that you are really absorbing what I'm talking about. The next time we meet, we're going to get into the number one solution for building a scalable business."

Exercise for the Reader:

Stop right now and spend thirty minutes planning out your business ideas. Start with where you want to be in five years. Next, lay out what you think you are going to need to get there. What systems do you need, what hires do you expect, and how are you going to leverage your time, which is your nonrenewable resource?

After you have spent time looking at which processes you want to put in place to grow your business over the next five years, take some time to break them down into concrete steps. Of these steps, which are the ones you absolutely must do yourself? Which steps can you outsource to others? Among the steps you can offload on others, who should do them? How much will it cost you to pay that person to do them? Can you hire someone cheaper? Can you automate them using technology?

CHAPTER 5:

Outsourcing to Take Back Your Life
(and Your Business)

Johnny reports to Sally, "I'm having a lot of difficulty examining all of the various systems within my practice. I'm trying to figure out what I can systematize. The problem is, how can I possibly do everything? I don't have enough of that nonrenewable resource, time. As I'm looking at all these things, it's becoming daunting to me. I'm looking at all of the various tasks I can systematize. I can create a system for that and a system for this. But now it looks like I have more to do than I had before. I get that outsourcing is important, but what should I be outsourcing and who should I be outsourcing it to?"

Sally replies, "You should be outsourcing everything that you can think of. Everything. This means administrative, marketing, investment management, and compliance, just to name a few. There are no limits to what you can outsource. The more you outsource, the more scalable your business will become. The more scalable your business becomes, the more money you can make, and the more time you'll have to spend on the critical tasks of building new relationships and deepening relationships with existing clients. Remember, outsourcing doesn't just mean using outsource vendors or outside vendors. It is also about outsourcing tasks off your plate to someone else within your firm. It could even be technology. Outsourcing is absolutely a key ingredient to building a scalable business."

Outsourcing is the number one solution for creating a scalable business. It's great to create systems and checklists, but the heavy lifting of creating a scalable business really involves outsourcing. Outsourcing has proven, through numerous studies, to help advisors build a more scalable business. We've talked about these statistics before, but I think they bears repeating because they're so critical to converting advisors who are do-it-yourselfers into turnkey advisors.

The Numbers

According to an SEI study,[19] those advisors who outsourced, compared to do-it-yourselfers, had 42 percent more clients and spent twice the amount of time in prospecting. They spend 85 percent more time in client meetings. They spent almost 50 percent more time marketing and advertising. However, the do-it-yourselfers spent 37 percent of their days on investment management functions, as opposed to those who outsourced and spent only 2 percent of their time on investment management functions. It's an incredible difference. Obviously, that's why they're able to spend 100 percent more of their time with prospects, 85 percent more of their time with existing clients, and 50% more time on marketing and advertising. It's a huge difference that translates into results. Those who are do-it-yourselfers are getting four new clients a year, versus turnkey advisors who get fourteen new clients a year, well over triple the number of new clients.

---

19 Anderson, Bueermann, and Lee, "A Data-Backed Solution to Building a More Profitable Advisory Business."

Areas to Outsource

You may not realize it, but you can outsource a number of areas; among them are investment management, administration, marketing, and compliance. Of these, the easiest area that you can outsource is investment management. Outsourcing investment management is a critical function that every scalable advisor should be taking advantage of because the results are in, and they reveal that, over time, this will be a way to create a much more scalable business, as well as a much more valuable business. You're going to acquire more clients, you're going to gather more assets, and the value of your firm will shoot way up. According to the study, over this ten-year period, the revenue of the firms increased by $1.8 million for those who outsourced investment management, versus a mere $800,000 increase in revenue for the do-it-yourselfers. In other words, there's a million-dollar difference in those who outsource investment management and those who do not.

Outsourcing investment management involves a number of key points. The first is that you must outsource to a firm that is easy to understand and explain. There are myriads of investment choices that a financial advisor can choose from that are good. They work. While they provide good results, they're often too difficult and complex for many advisors to explain, and thus too difficult and complex for many clients to understand. While it may seem counter-intuitive, it does you no good to find an investment management solution for your practice that is too complex to understand or too complex to explain, regardless of how good the results are.

The second point to keep in mind is that the solutions you outsource need to be scalable among all of your various client categories. As an example, you may have young clients who are a little bit more aggressive because they have more time until retirement. You may also have middle-aged clients who are less aggressive and have a lower risk tolerance. In addition, you're going to have retirees that are really low on the aggression scale and just need income. Clearly, you don't want to go out and find overly complicated solutions that are different for everybody. Instead, you want to pick three to five good solutions that you can intermix among your clients.

Just for simplicity's sake, we're going to choose three different solutions—a tactical manager, a strategic manager, and a fixed income manager. The product mix between those three can be used for all of our clients, from the aggressive to the moderate to the conservative clients, but in different proportions. We may choose to use no fixed income for our aggressive clients; It may be a fifty-fifty blend between tactical and strategic. As we move down the risk spectrum, we may increase the tactical and fixed income allocation while decreasing the strategic allocation. The key point is that we use only three managers in different allocations for the bulk of our clients.

Rather than having five options for aggressive clients, five completely different options for moderate clients, and five completely different options for conservative clients, try to choose three to five options that can be used for all your clients, but in different proportions. This approach is important for a scalable business because not only does it create simplicity in your business, but it also creates ease of client interaction. Imagine if you had five different solutions for your three different categories, and three to five different categories of clients, then you'd have fifteen to twenty-five solutions you're using with your clients and you've got to know about all of those solutions, as opposed to using three to five in various mixes and proportions with your clients. This way, you'll only need to know these three to five solutions.

When a client calls, I am able to see that he is 27-years-old and a younger professional. I know he's going to be best served by a mix of two products. On the other hand, if a retiree calls me, I know the three products he's in, and I know them inside and out.

I would urge all the advisors reading this book to create deep relationships with their outsourced investment management solutions. You can't develop those deep relationships amongst a broad array of products—you need to keep it simple for your practice if you want to create a scalable business. We see some advisors that use twenty-five different products, fifty different products, or 100 different products, and their business is not scalable. It may be effective for their clients, but it is not scalable. The good news is that you can be both effective and scalable. Some advisors believe that creating more complexity is a core part of their value proposition, which it is not. The clients simply do not care about the level of complexity. The average client does not know a lot about how markets operate. They just want someone they trust to offer them clear suggestions about where to put their money so they can achieve their financial goals. As a matter of fact, they don't like levels of complexity. They typically prefer simplicity and value good service—That is how they judge their advisors. I have never seen a survey in which a client has said, "We rank our advisors based on the level of complexity of their investment solutions." That is simply never an answer given by clients.

The other three areas to outsource solutions that are easy and simple to implement include administration, marketing, and compliance. For most advisors who have broker dealers, their compliance function is already outsourced to their broker dealer. They are giving up some of their payout to their broker dealer, specifically to cover things like their compliance. Among those firms that don't have a broker dealer, such as independent Registered Investment Advisors (RIAs), they must find an outsourced compliance solution. Outsourcing your compliance solution is very important—this is an area that you do not want to try yourself, due to its complexity and ever-changing rules, regulations, and requirements. It is essential as an independent financial advisor with no broker dealer affiliation to find an outsourced compliance solution.

As far as administration goes, you can outsource many of your administrative functions to a myriad of firms. These out sourced administative solutions can input data into customer relationship management software. They can research prospect names. They can gather information from various websites. They can scan documents for you. There is a plethora of solutions when it comes to outsourcing any kind of administrative functions (or really any functions) within your firm, from website creation and administration to social media. I would highly recommend using Upwork.com. Upwork is a tremendous solution for outsourcing almost anything, from writing newsletters to designing websites, creating logos, conducting research, and basically just about anything one can imagine. I have introduced numerous financial advisors to Upwork, and once they learn about it, they find that they cannot live without it. It is a fantastic tool for financial advisors to use to outsource their administration and many other tasks in a very cost-effective manner.

Additionally, many advisors have found they can outsource virtually all of their marketing. There are entire firms that will help you build marketing campaigns, make the calls, and set appointments. These firms will send out all your seminar invites. A few firms out there are really good in this area. One is called White Glove, and another is called Snappy Kraken. Those are two firms that we've seen advisors use for outsourcing some of their marketing functions, but Upwork.com is another place that you can use for outsourcing stuff like social media posts. There are social media experts on Upwork that will do posts for you. They'll do social media research. They'll do internet research. They'll generate leads for you. They will even make calls for you. Upwork is a solution with very broad applications. You can find anyone to do almost anything within your practice on Upwork.

Most financial advisors who are interested in conducting outbound call campaigns simply do not have enough time to make hundreds of calls on a weekly basis to prospects. This is prime outsourcing material.

One strong solution in this area is a company called Fancy Hands, which is a solid outbound call option I have seen work.

A Case Study

To summarize, outsourcing is the source for creating a scalable practice. One of my good friends has a $100 million plus practice on his own. He has no other advisors working for him. He has nobody working full-time for him. He has outsourced everything. He's a standalone RIA. He doesn't have any broker dealer affiliation, but he outsources his marketing, his social media, his administration, his compliance, and his investment management. He outsources it all. All he does is relationship management. He builds deep relationships with his clients. It's a tremendous practice. He never loses clients that he doesn't fire. He's a perfect example of what outsourcing can do to the nth degree, and he has a tremendously scalable practice. He could easily add another couple hundred million dollars to his business without hiring anybody. He'll spend more money on outsourcing, absolutely, but he has no personnel issues. He has no overhead issues. He has a beautiful office, and he doesn't have to worry about any of the stuff that a lot of advisors do who don't outsource. He started all of that with outsourcing his investment management function. Once he caught the outsourcing bug, he started looking at every other area in his business that he could outsource, and he's never looked back.

Just think what outsourcing could do for you.

"After hearing all that, I should be outsourcing," Johnny says. "I cannot wait to begin the process. How should I start?"

Sally replies, "Simply go back to the list you made when we last spoke, analyze what can you outsource, and what must you do personally. In the end, you should have a list of all the tasks and all the systems. Once you have this list, put notes next to each of the items—"outsource, me, outsource, me," and so on. With luck, there will be more "outsources" than "me"s.

"Every time you write a 'me,'" she continued, "stop and try to see if you can figure out a way you can turn that 'me' into an outsource. Next, figure out where you're going to outsource these tasks to. It could be to technology, it could be to your current home office, it could be to an investment management company, it could be to an outside vendor, or it could be to a freelancer like you'd find through Upwork. Every single one of those outsources must have with it a tag as to where you're going to actually outsource it to." She said with a chuckle, "As a note, Johnny, this is classic 'working-on-your-business' stuff."

> ## Exercise for the Reader:
>
> Spend fifteen to thirty minutes writing and thinking about what specific tasks you can outsource. Can you outsource appointment setting, social media posts, newsletter writing, portfolio management, or paperwork? List everything possible, not just those areas you want to outsource. Remember, just because you may enjoy a certain task and want to keep doing it instead of outsourcing it, this does not mean that is the correct thing to do for your business or your work-life balance.

CHAPTER 6:

A Systematic Approach to Creating Systems

Sally starts the meeting as she and Johnny sit down by asking, "How did you do with your outsourcing list?"

Johnny replies, "Pretty good. What I found is that I can basically outsource everything."

She gives him a quizzical look. "Everything?"

"Well, not quite everything. I realized the one thing I cannot outsource is relationship development. I need to be the one meeting with my clients. I am the one to hold their hand. I am the one that needs to return their calls when they call me, but basically everything else I can and should outsource if I'm going to create a scalable business. But I have a problem with outsourcing, and I think it's a big problem."

"So, what's the big problem?" Sally asks.

"I worry the quality of work will suffer if someone else is creating a plan, doing the paperwork, gathering data for a plan, or creating follow-up notes. How can I be sure that my clients and prospects are getting the best possible service if I'm not involved?"

"It's funny you say that, Johnny. This is exactly what my worry was, and it was the reason it took me a while to build a scalable business. Fortunately, it is easy to deal with. All you've got to do is to create pilots."

"What on earth are you talking about?" Johnny says.

"Johnny, think about it. Pilots have very little room for error, yet they make hundreds of small decisions daily. The quality of the work must be top notch. Their decisions must be the same every time—they all must be consistent, and all of their work must be done with no mistakes. They do all of this by following systems, and the key to systems is checklists," Sally replies.

Developing Systems

Whereas Chapter 5 described the philosophical essence of scalability, outsourcing, Chapter 6 contains the nuts-and-bolts center of scalability. While, we've talked about what we need to outsource, the time we can save, and the efficiencies we can create by outsourcing, Chapter 6 now looks at how we actually develop systems within our firm that put all of this stuff together while still providing high-quality, consistent and thorough service for our clients.

Chapter 6 is all about creating systems. How do we create systems? What's the essence of systems? What are the steps for creating systems? What are some of the dos and don'ts of creating systems? Many of the key principles discussed in this particular chapter are centered around the work of Atul Gawande and his book, *The Checklist Manifesto*.[20] *The Checklist Manifesto* relates that the problem that we have today isn't information or the lack of information. It's that we have too much information. What this has done is created mental overload in many of the tasks that we try to complete in our daily lives, especially in our professional lives. Additionally, Gawande relates that the solution to this mental overload is checklists. There are numerous examples of this discussed in *The Checklist Manifesto*. We can see how checklists have

---

20 Gawande, *The Checklist Manifesto: How to Get Things Right.*

absolutely transformed the medical and aviation field, and how they can do the same for the financial advisory industry.

Checklists are a critical component of creating effective systems. A checklist provides a safeguard against faulty memory, distractions, and skipped steps. When we deal with something as complex as a client's financial plan, there are so many different areas that we could skip by accident, or forget about. As a result, we need to make sure that we have checklists that verify that we haven't neglected any important areas and also encourage consistent high standards when we're dealing with clients. A checklist will help you create this consistency.

Attributes of Good Checklists

A common problem is that people who create checklists have a tendency to lean towards complexity. They feel that if their checklist is not "thorough," it's not going to work. Actually, the opposite is true. Effective checklists and systems, have three attributes in common. They're simple, they're measurable, and they're transmissible, meaning they're duplicatable. Even in the most complex of spaces, such in the aerospace or medical industries, the more complex the checklist was, the more failures users had in implementing the checklist. As a result, workers in those industries are now encouraged to create checklists that are much simpler. A checklist should only have between six and nine items before hitting a natural pause. Financial advisors may utilize multiple checklists, but every checklist needs to contain only six to nine items and be printed on only one sheet of paper. The idea is that it's very simple, and anybody can do it. It's transferrable. It's duplicatable.

As an example, we may have a specific checklist of items that we're going to cover for our first meeting with clients. After going through six to nine items with a new client, there should be a natural pause. It is important to look at where the natural pauses emerge. We may have a separate checklist for retirement plans. We may have a separate checklist for insurance. We may have a separate checklist for legacy planning. We may have several different checklists that we cover with our clients during the various meetings. Remember, they are not lumped all together into one giant checklist. We don't have this giant, forty-seven-item checklist that we're going to go through with our clients. We may eventually go through forty-seven items, but we're not doing it all at once. We have a simple checklist. Once the first checklist is done, we move to the next checklist.

Checklists are the absolute core of creating systems. You cannot have systems without a checklist. It doesn't work that way. There's too much complexity. You're going to screw up. It's absolutely critical that as an advisor you create systems, which is the essence of creating a scalable business. Specifically, these systems must have checklists, and quite honestly, everyone who wants to scale their business should read *The Checklist Manifesto*.

Keep in mind the goal of creating systems is to create consistent processes for your business and clients. The essence of creating these systems is the creation of checklists. The checklist is the central part that actually creates this consistency.

When we look at an advisory practice, when we look at scalability, when we look at developing systems, we've got to look at all of the processes that occur within our business.

We have to look at our business like a factory. How do we get a new client from point A to point Z? What are all the steps that we need to complete to move the client from point A to point Z? Those steps are the processes we need to document. What are all the processes that that client needs to go through to turn them into an ideal client? It's important, when we look at the scalable advisor, that they're looking at their business from a global viewpoint. This echoes a point I made earlier in Chapter 4—that it is very important that the scalable advisor spends time working on their business, instead of always working in their business. One of the key points of working on their business is determining what all of these specific processes are. Think of a scalable business as a factory; you can't create a factory by just looking at the roof. You've got to look at all the things that are going on inside that factory and determine what the processes and systems are to create a successful outcome.

There are processes for marketing. There are processes for client development. There are processes for paperwork. There are processes for social media. There are processes for getting referrals. There are processes for following up with clients. There are processes for dealing with negative issues with clients. A scalable advisor needs to look at all of the processes within their business, and how they're getting clients from this point to that point, or dealing with this issue to that issue.

As financial advisors, we may have processes for attracting a new client, onboarding a new client, and prospecting, marketing, and social media. We may have a process for how we deal with client complaints. We should have a process for how we deal with client updates on an annual basis, and for client reviews. This list provides us with a blueprint for all of the different checklists that we need to create to ensure the consistency of our processes. The key to running a business that is process-oriented is using checklists to ensure we don't ever skip a step. We can have a high-volume business, and still provide the same high-level customer experience that clients are yearning for.

Identifying processes is one of the key steps that an advisor needs to do when they're analyzing how to move toward a scalable advisory practice. The processes and checklists will then get us to consistency. If we identify the processes that we run to get a client from A to Z, when new clients come in, every client will go through the same processes. Now that we have created a checklist, we are sure to provide a consistent and thorough process and experience for our clients. Checklists mean that we don't overlook something. We don't skip a step. We don't forget about anything. It's always the same experience and process for every client.

The Value of Checklists

The final piece to this puzzle is that, by using checklists and systems, we're able to use the lowest dollar denominated individual, skillset, or outsourced service to run through the different processes and different checklists. As an example, without a checklist, I probably couldn't have my sales assistants run a lot of the meetings with my clients because they're not as experienced as me. They're going to forget things. They're not going to even know about things. But if I was able to give a not-very-experienced, newer sales assistant a checklist of items to cover with a client, I know when they're done, they followed the checklist. I know that the client experience they'll have is as close as possible to the experience they'd have with me. As a note, I would probably have a less-experienced individual gather the basic information, but I would personally be the one getting into the nitty gritty of their financial situation.

Now, my business is not just scalable from the viewpoint of the ability to outsource tasks to other people within my practice, but it's also scalable because it is duplicatable. I now know the system to move a prospect to a client, which is what makes our business money, and I now know that system is in place with clearly thought-out processes, and well-documented checklists. This means that anyone I bring on board can follow that system to move a client through this process in a consistent and thorough manner, which, in turn, generates revenue for our firm.

To reiterate—checklists, systems, and processes build consistency in the business. They build scalability in the business because I can outsource various tasks and various processes to different people within my organization, and they create a scalable business because now my business is duplicatable. I can have other people do the same thing, build a business in the manner that I feel is appropriate for our clients and for our client experience, without having to worry about their actually doing it correctly because they are now following the system, they're following the processes, they're following the checklists, and our clients are getting a consistent, thorough experience.

Checklists also have a side benefit in that most people enjoy crossing items off of them. Studies have shown that checking items off a list releases endorphins in your brain. There's a mini-high that you get that's a result of physiological processes that occur in the brain when we complete steps on a checklist and cross them off. It is its own reward.

Johnny says, "I feel so much better about outsourcing now that I realize that I can create systems for everything. And these checklists should cover not only the things I want to outsource, but everything else in my business that I might want someone to take over. That includes what I do personally. Everything within my financial advisory business must have a specific checklist system created for it. Sally, this seems like a daunting and time-consuming task."

"It is daunting and it is time-consuming, but it is also worth it. This process of making checklists is actually about two things: working on your business instead of in your business and time. Are you going to invest time or spend time? When you work on your business, you are investing time. When you work in your business, you're often just spending time," Sally says.

"But where do I start?" Johnny says.

"That's an excellent question. There are really three primary functions of your business and therefore three primary systems you need to develop. The first is generating leads. How do you market your business? The second is turning leads into clients. How do you get them to say yes? And third is turning clients into fans. How do you create a self-perpetuating business with raving fans?"

Exercise for the Reader:

Take time to list all the processes that you can think of that take place in your business. Then look at each one and break it down into the steps that you take in order to accomplish these processes. What can you create a checklist for? Remember, each checklist should contain no more than six to nine items. If you have a checklist that contains more than nine items, see if you can identify sub-processes within the larger process. Then write a checklist for each sub process.

For example, one checklist I've seen used by other successful advisors looks like this:

Important Financial Documents Checklist

When you meet with a financial planner, you will probably be asked to bring the following types of documents. These documents, along with the Personal Data Organizer will be used to tailor a financial plan to meet your life goals.

Retirement Planning Documents

- ☐ Recent IRA, 401(k), 403(b), TSA, Keogh statements
- ☐ Employee benefits program
- ☐ Deferred compensation and stock option agreements
- ☐ Pension and profit sharing statements

Tax Planning Documents

- ☐ Tax returns for last year
- ☐ W-2 and a recent pay stub
- ☐ Estimated taxes

Financial Documents

- ☐ Savings account statements
- ☐ Mutual fund statements
- ☐ Brokerage account statements
- ☐ Investment documents
- ☐ Loan documents
- ☐ List of stocks held outside of brokerages
- ☐ Partnership agreements

Asset Protection Documents

- ☐ Life insurance policies and statements
- ☐ Medical, homeowners and auto insurance policies and statements
- ☐ Disability, umbrella, and long term care insurance policies
- ☐ Annuity policies and statements

Estate Planning Documents

- ☐ Summary of your will, living will, durable powers of attorney and health care powers
- ☐ Living trusts

CHAPTER 7

Generating Leads

Johnny asks Sally, "Where should we start in creating systems?" She replies, "System #1 should be a system for creating leads. How do we get people to raise their hands?"

"That definitely makes sense," Johnny says. "Generating leads is incredibly important, but it's also something that I've struggled with terribly over the years. How do I get more people to talk to?"

Sally says, "Believe me, you are preaching to choir on this one. When I got in the business, there were only four ways that people were using to generate leads. The first was the old-school way of using the white pages, or, as we called it, smiling and dialing, which doesn't work well anymore. Number two is friends and family. Having conversations with these kinds of referrals can be awkward, especially for a new advisor. The third way that people were generating leads was with seminars, but they were expensive and produced spotty results, at best. And the fourth way, which seems like what most people do, is the 'do everything' way. I call it the 'everything bagel' way. It is networking. It is friends and family. It's putting on webinars, it's handing out business cards, it's going to networking events. It's whatever it takes to try to get business. It's really an 'anything goes and just hope something works' strategy. This shotgun approach is not good at generating a reliable and consistent stream of new leads.

Johnny says, laughingly, "It's funny, since the 'do everything' approach describes me to a T. As a matter of fact, that's where I first met you—at one of the five networking events I go to every week."

Sally says, "In developing a system for generating leads, let's go over some absolutely critical areas that you must consider."

Chapter 7 is about generating leads. When I say generating leads, all you're looking for people to do is to raise their hands. In looking at a sea of people, I like to visualize those who are raising their hand saying, "Tell me more." That is what we are looking to accomplish. How do we get people to raise their hands? Even before we even get them to raise their hands, it's important for us to be positioned properly so we get the right hands raised. This relates to specialization. Specialization is another critical component of the scalable financial advisory practice.

Reasons for Specializing

There are a number of reasons for specializing. Number one is it focuses what your market is and the knowledge base you need to possess so as to serve that specific market. This morning I may get a military officer as a client, this afternoon I have a government employee as a client, then the next day I have an entrepreneur as a client, and the day after that I have a divorced woman as a client. All of these are specific kinds of clients who have specific subject matter knowledge bases that I need to know in depth so as to adequately serve them.

The problem with most advisors is that they try to be all things to all people, and that's impossible to do. Instead, they need to be specialized. In looking at specialization, it's important to become a subject matter expert. I'll use divorced women as an example because I have seen several advisors who have a specialty in this particular niche.

How did they get into that specialty? First, they typically found they had the right kind of empathetic personality for this particular group, but, more importantly, they all decided that they wanted to become the most in-depth subject matter expert on the needs of divorced women.

One challenge they found was that many of the women that they worked with—not all,—but many, didn't have a firm grasp of all the financial decisions that were taking place in he marriage prior to the divorce. As a result, they didn't know about their life insurance needs and they didn't understand the retirement choices that they'd been making over the years; they didn't fully grasp all the decisions that had been made in their financial plan. Many of these ladies were middle aged or getting closer to their end retirement goals, yet they often lacked confidence in making critical financial decisions. The advisors found the need to get these clients educated and comfortable enough to make these important decisions, all while going through what is often a bad emotional time for them due to the divorce.

They all became subject matter experts on how to speak with women during this often difficult period in their lives. They found it was especially important to pay close attention to the emotional side of the business. Serving them well meant they needed to become an expert at not only at explaining the technical steps of what they needed to do to separate their insurance policies and financial plans from those of their ex-spouse, but it was even more important for them to grasp the emotional significance of what they were going through and how to support their clients in what can be moments of emotional crisis and difficulty.

You can become a subject matter expert through creating training programs, through creating seminars, or through writing articles or blog posts in that specific area of specialization. What groups do you want to serve? Whether you choose government employees, divorced women, military officers, small business owners, or some other specific group of people that you feel an affinity for, there are industry associations that advisors who cater to that particular population can join to get even more intimately involved in that group's culture. For example, join dental associations for focusing on dental clients, join military associations if you are focusing on military personnel, or there are thousands of other different associations associated with different specialties that a financial advisor can land upon. By having a specialization, you can relax in knowing you have just this population that you are focused on—just focus on these specific groups, these specific associations, these specific members. That way, you don't have to join all of the possible groups and try to be a jack of all trades. In building a scalable practice, specialization is a very important component.

Another benefit of specialization is that financial advisors can network with centers of influence within that specialty. As with the example of working with divorced women clients as a specialty, divorce lawyers have also been a great center of influence that financial advisors were able to network with because that's exactly who they're dealing with as well. Having a financial advisor who focuses on the special needs of women getting divorced was absolutely important for these clients over time, their lawyers saw how beneficial it was to their clients to have a financial advisor who understood the uniqueness of this specific market niche.

Among many couples, a relationship with a financial advisor has traditionally been between the husband and the financial advisor. This is starting to change, thank goodness, but that doesn't erase the history of the profession. The reason is that the majority of financial advisors are men, which has been the case for a long time. Many things financial advisors typically do with their clients have been associated with traditionally masculine activities: going golfing or to the car dealership. By having someone who focused specifically on divorced women, there was someone who was listening to the woman's needs, versus what the men were dictating. In other words, if you can identify a group that has not been traditionally well-served by our profession, and you feel empathy toward members of that group, it might be a good population to consider specializing in serving.

Another reason specialization helps financial advisors is that it allows them to mine networking groups specifically for leads. If you walk in and say, "I'm a financial advisor, and I work with high-net-worth clients," that's great, but you're not painting a very clear picture of your ideal client for the networking group to give you referrals. However, if you come into the networking group and say, "I work with senior federal employees dealing with the intricacies of their unique financial plans or the unique retirement systems only available to senior federal employees," you've painted a picture of exactly what you do. In other areas you may say, "I specialize in military officers, I specialize in divorced women, or I specialize in pharmacists." That's all you do. You do not work with anyone else; just pharmacists. This allows you to paint a picture specifically of those individuals that you're looking to raise their hand and say, "Tell me more about your practice."

Always think about this: What is the niche that you can dominate? That's what you're looking at when you're deciding what area you're going to specialize in. It's not enough, again, to be a jack of all trades and a master of none. You've got to have a clear specialty if you want to have a scalable practice. This is going to allow you to build a deep knowledge base in that area of expertise, which is absolutely critical, as opposed to trying to know something about everything. You need to actually know everything about one thing. That's the important element when it comes to specialization.

The Role of Specialization in Generating Leads

When it comes to looking at specifically getting prospects to raise their hands and say "tell me more," an excellent book called *The Purple Cow* by Seth Godin[21] was very influential to me and my marketing life. Seth is a marketing guru. The premise of *The Purple Cow* is that when we drive down a rural road, we often see cows. The first cow might be memorable, but after a while they all just blend in. Eventually, you do not even pay

---

21 Seth Godin, *The Purple Cow: Transform Your Business by Being Remarkable* (New York, NY: Portfolio, 2009).

attention to the hundreds of cows we see everywhere out there, because they all look the same. But imagine if you saw a purple cow. You would remember that—it would stand out.

The premise of this book is you've got to be the purple cow. How do you make your business the purple cow? One of those ways is by specialization. I'm not the advisor who does everything for everybody; I'm the advisor who focuses on dentists, and that's it. I know about dentistry, I know about your terminology, I know what kind of hours you work, I understand what your schooling involved. I understand this niche inside and out. That is one way to become the purple cow. We're going to talk about more ways to become the purple cow later, when it comes to WOW service, but for now, think about specialization as an important step in developing the purple cow practice.

Another thing that Seth Godin talks about is pertinent to intangible businesses. The financial services business is largely intangible. You're selling these very abstract products that nobody can touch. But your marketing is one of the tangibles that clients actually get to see and feel, so it's important that you have something that stands out in that area. I probably have thousands (not a thousand, but thousands) of business cards from financial advisors as a sea of regular cows. Among those, only a few stand out (the purple cows). When I find a great one, I think, "Wow, that's unique. It says something unique, it feels unique, it has a unique size, it's unique in its shape, it's unique in its coloring. It's not just the same old: "Here's my phone number, here's my picture, here's a logo, here's an email address, and on the back is my broker dealer." It is something unique; it is a purple cow. This is just a small example of how to stand out, but Seth Godin feels it is an important one for intangible businesses.

Think about every interaction that your potential customers, your potential prospects, have with you. Is it purple cow? Is it standing out amongst the sea? If I litter my table with business cards, as an example, does yours stand out as a purple cow? Every interaction needs to be the purple cow to get people to come to you, to raise their hand, to ask for more information.

Advisors also need to understand that content is a major driver in getting folks to raise their hands. It's not just the fact that I exist that's going to get prospects to raise their hands—many advisors believe if they have a better mouse trap, prospects are going to raise their hand. You need content that is going to get people to raise their hands. Look at your website. Is it purple cow? Is it engaging? Is it talking about your specialty in a way that speaks to that specific niche? On social media—Facebook, LinkedIn, and Twitter—are you engaged in all three platforms or any other platforms? Does your target client population use Instagram? You need to tailor your offerings so that your niche market is seeing that information and has an opportunity to raise their hand. Do you have a newsletter that speaks to your specialization? Are you sending out emails regularly to your existing clients and to your prospects? Are you doing webinars or seminars that focus on your specific market niche?

One of our advisors focuses on Certified Public Accountants, which is interesting because a lot of CPAs are actually giving financial advice in many areas within their accounting practice. But they need financial advisors of their own. What this advisor did was create a continuing education course for CPAs; all CPAs must have a certain number of hours every year for continuing education. He created a free continuing education course on financial planning for CPAs. He's providing this content for free to get CPAs to eventually raise their hand afterwards to say, "Hey, I need to know more about that. I didn't know that. Tell me more."

Radio shows and podcasts are probably the king of the content providers. We've seen many top producers use radio shows to deliver content to a very broad spectrum. Radio shows are not necessary for success, but we see a lot of the top producers using radio for the delivery of their content. It is expensive; it's a wide net you are casting, but it does work.

Regardless of how you are reaching prospects, just know that the right content will get prospects to raise their hand. Some delivery mechanisms are broader, some are more targeted, and some are more expensive. You need to determine what the right medium is for you. It may be a combination of several, and you may need to try a couple before you land on what is effective for you, your content, and your intended audience.

Sizzle and Steak

There are two areas that content must speak to, and I call them the steak and the sizzle. The sizzle is what's going to get their attention. The sizzle is what's going to get them to say, "I want to read more about this, or I want to open this email." A subject line is sizzle, a headline is sizzle.

The steak is what's going to justify to them to keep reading more, but you have to make sure you have both the sizzle and the steak. It can't be all sex appeal—You need substance behind it. Newsletters are a perfect example of a medium that a lot of advisors utilize. I find that most newsletters I read are full of steak; There is little to no sizzle. You've got to have sizzle in every interaction with your client or prospective client. You want them to ask for more information, to read more, to open something, to forward something, and so on.

Fundamentally, there are only five reasons as to why someone will raise their hand—when you are creating your content, think about these five reasons. They are fear, need, greed, friendship, or curiosity. You need to be speaking to those five areas. You've got to be thinking about what their fear is. What are their needs? What's their greed? "You can earn this kind of interest rate." That's a greed thing. Losing money in the stock market or not being able to retire, that plays to the fear angle. A need example would be wanting to retire at sixty-five or needing a specific retirement income. And how can you participate in the stock market, but still protect against devastating losses? This speaks to a client's curiosity.

All of your content needs to be crafted with at least one of those five core reasons in mind. Then, you must filter your content through two words, and the two words are, "So what?" You should look at everything you write, every email you write, every subject line you write, every article you write in your newsletter, every Facebook post, through the lens of "So what?" If you can't answer that question, eliminate that bit of your content. How important is it? You have to filter everything for importance and the impact that it is having with your clients or your prospects. "So what?" is the filter to accomplish this goal.

The final way to generate leads is referrals. Referrals are a great way to generate leads. But you cannot just hope for referrals; you have to develop a system for getting referrals. A great book that addresses this point is *Expecting Referrals* by Scott Kramnick.[22] It provides a lot of little nuggets on how to develop and lay the groundwork for expecting referrals in every one of your interactions with your clients and prospects, so that when it comes to actually asking for referrals in the end, it's completely expected for them to give a referral, and it doesn't become an awkward conversation.

Johnny says, "This way of thinking is still difficult for me, as I'm afraid if I specialize in a specific niche, I'll be losing clients."

Sally says, You will, and that's actually exactly what you want. You do not want to be all things to all people. You cannot build a successful scalable business that way. I would say this—spend some time looking at your book of business and really analyze what clients you like working with best and what clients you like working with least. Don't think about the economics of the relationship during this initial analysis. This little exercise is a great way to begin developing your niche specialization.

---

[22] Scott A. Kramnick, *Expecting Referrals: The Resurrection of a Lost Art* (Fredericksburg, Va.: Associates Publishing, 1993).

You then need to brainstorm as to what content is going to get them to raise their hands and say, "Tell ME MORE!" Your content has to have sizzle and steak. Speak to the five primary reasons for them to raise their hand and pay attention: Need, Greed, Fear, Curiosity and Friendship."

Exercise for the Reader:

Think about a population for whom you'd like to serve as financial advisor. Bonus points if it's a population that traditionally has not been adequately served by the financial services sector. What needs do they have that are different from the average population? If you're not sure, or even if you think you already know, what groups can you join that will help you learn more about their needs? What kind of financial products do you know of that are specifically tailored to this group? Put yourself in this population's shoes. What kind of help and support would matter most to you?

CHAPTER 8:
Turning Leads into Clients

Johnny says, "I think I have a grasp of what I need to do in order to create a lead generation machine, but I worry about what will happen if I get a bunch of leads, but I'm not able to follow up with them all. Some will fall through the cracks, and we won't get the business we expected to get from all the leads that we generate. So, we spend all this money or all of this time on some sort of fantastic lead generation system, but in the end, I generate too much, and I'm not going to be able to follow up with them all."

"Your worry is not unfounded," Sally says. "In fact, this is a huge problem with a lot of advisors. It's not that they're creating too many leads, but that they create their leads inconsistently, then follow up with them inconsistently. They have a bunch of leads, but not enough time to follow up with them or, more often than not, they don't have the right system to follow up with them. The solution to this problem is the same solution to every one of these problems—systems. You must have a clear system of how you are going to turn leads into clients. How are you going to get them to say yes to working with you, to implementing your provided plan, and to becoming a part of your business?"

Johnny hesitantly says, "I'm not about closing or hard selling."

Sally replies, "Neither am I. I came from a non-sales background. What I'm about is a process; a specific, step-by-step system that takes prospects along a journey from education, to gathering information, to analysis, to the delivery of plan, and eventually, the implementation of the plan. I'm leaving a little bit out by over-simplifying, but let me explain in a bit more detail."

Turning Leads into Clients

This chapter focuses on turning leads into clients. This is probably where the rubber meets the road in building the business. All the other steps leading up to this include questions such as, "How do we position our business? How do we structure our business?" But the actual stage that's going to build our business is turning our leads into clients. We can generate all the leads we want, but if we don't have a systematic process for turning them into clients, we have nothing.

In this chapter, we're going to talk about that systematic process, and it's going to include a lot of parts. It's going to include specific systems, it's going to include specific checklists, and it's going to include specific steps. The key to all of this is that you, the advisor, need to create a multi-step process that begins with education, that leads into information gathering, that leads into analysis, that leads into recommendations, and that leads into leads turning into clients. We are going to discuss the various phases of how to do this. I break the sales process into six specific phases of turning a lead into a client.

The Six Phases

Phase one is the education phase. This phase can easily take an hour or more. Among advisors that have a high persistency of business, they always have a major education component to their sales process. Those advisors with low persistency have little to no education process when it comes to turning leads into clients. Based on this fact, I have concluded that education is an absolute critical step that cannot be overlooked. You cannot shortcut education, and it easily can take an hour or more.

There are seven different areas that need to be covered during the education process. The first three concepts—diversification, the S&P 500, and asset allocation—all have to do with how the portfolio is going to be initially structured. The next three—systematic risk, the math of losses, and risk management—are all going into how we take the asset allocation portfolio and create a risk management overlay on that portfolio.

Clients should be taught the power of diversification. They need to understand how diversification can help manage risk. A key concept with regard to diversification is correlation. The key to building a diversified portfolio is ensuring that the building blocks being used do things at different times for different reasons. We can mathematically measure this difference, and it is correlation. It does not matter how many pieces we have in our portfolio. You can have twenty different mutual funds, and you may still not be diversified. If all twenty of those mutual funds are moving at the same time for similar reasons, they are correlated, and you are not diversified. Clients MUST understand what diversification actually is, and they also need to understand what diversification is not.

Which leads to the second key component that must be covered in the education phase—discussing what the S&P 500 is. A lot of advisors will ask, "Why do we need to even cover that? We're not investing our client in the S&P 500." However, the S&P 500 is what the vast majority of clients are going to get bombarded with from the media and their friends as the bellwether of the market. So, clients need to understand what the S&P 500 is and what it is not, and the key is they need to understand that the S&P 500 is not a well-balanced, diversified portfolio of 500 stocks. It simply is not. It is heavily weighted to several sectors and to a handful of specific stocks. It is not a well-diversified vehicle. Clients need to understand that if they are going to try to use the S&P 500 as a comparative as to how they're doing with their financial advisor; it's an apples and orange comparison. They really need to understand right up front what the S&P 500 is and what it is not.

The third concept to educate our prospects and clients on is asset allocation and modern portfolio theory. Clearly, this builds upon the diversification discussion. Asset allocation is just the practical application of a diversified portfolio. Nobel prizes have been awarded around the concept of asset allocation and modern portfolio theory. It is really the core tenet for how scalable advisors are going to build effective and intellectually defensible portfolios for their clients.

The fourth concept in the education phase that needs to be covered is what systematic risk is. Asset allocation is fine and dandy about 90 percent of the time, maybe even more than that. However, the 5 to 10 percent of the time that asset allocation is not good is when the market has systematic risk issues. Investopedia defines systematic risk as the risk inherent to the entire market, also known as "undiversifiable risk." Interest rates, recession, and wars all represent sources of systematic risk because they affect the entire market and cannot be avoided through diversification.

The crash of 2008 is a very good example of systematic risk. It almost didn't matter where you were during 2008. You may not have been down 40 plus percent like the market, but you were down probably 20, 25, or 30 percent. Systematic risk is an absolute critical component to cover because a lot of advisors and clients believe asset allocation is the end answer. Asset allocation is definitely part of the answer, but asset allocation does not address systematic risk, and clients have to understand this and prepare their portfolios and financial plans for systematic risk.

Number five is that clients must understand the mathematical concept that losses are more powerful than gains. They need to understand that losses have a greater mathematic impact on portfolio results than the mathematic impact of gains. The reason clients must understand this concept is that many clients believe that gains and losses have the same impact on portfolio results. As an example, let's say I have $100,000. It goes up 50 percent and then down 50 percent. Many clients intuitively would say, "If it goes up 50 before going down 50, I probably break even." Actually, you lose 25 percent; you now only have $75,000.

In other words, losses are not equal to gains. Losses are much more powerful than gains. They have a greater impact on portfolio results, as opposed to the impact of gains. Clients need to understand this fact because they must value loss prevention. If they do not understand the value of loss prevention, they are always going to want to take risks to try and capture all of the ups and gains in the market, which we do not need to do if we are able to prevent some of the losses. If we can prevent the catastrophic losses, we do not have to take all of the risks trying to get all of the upside in the market. If we position our portfolios to attempt to participate in all of the upside of the market, we are typically then exposed to all of the downside of the market.

The sixth topic that clients need to understand is risk management. Advisors need to consider two areas of risk management. The first is the risk management of their clients' portfolios. As discussed above, we must mitigate the risk of catastrophic losses, so that we do not have the math of losses working against us. The second is the insurance area of risk management, which basically means insuring against the risks of life. This includes disability insurance, life insurance, liability insurance, and long-term care insurance. Clients must be educated about risk management overlays on their portfolios and all of the various insurance concepts and products that may be needed to insure the various risks they are potentially facing in their financial future.

The seventh basic concept in the education phase is emotions. Clients should be taught how emotions may drive them to make poor decisions. We call this the behavioral coaching area, so we want to show them some examples of what happens when we let the emotions drive our decision making.

A good example occurred during the 2007 - 2009 bear market that we all experienced. The maximum buying was near the peak of the bull market before it crashed, and the maximum selling was near the bottom of the bear market. In other words, clients, generally speaking, were buying high and selling low, which is exactly the opposite of what they should be doing, and that was because of emotions. They're excited when the market's at the top, and they buy in, or they're depressed when the market's at the bottom, and they sell out. A wise advisor once said that clients are wired to do the wrong things at the wrong times, and an advisor's job is simply to prevent this emotional reaction and instead get them to do the right things at the right times.

By educating clients about the emotional roller coaster ahead of time, you are inoculating them against poor emotional decisions later on. At least you will have a reference to point back to and say, "Remember when we discussed the emotional roller coaster? Well, you are on it right now. Let's talk about what you want to do and see if it makes sense in light of your entire financial plan."

Standardizing the Process

In phase one of turning leads into clients, we need to make sure that we have a standard process to follow up with for every new client. The education process we're using should cover all these different topics in a standardized way, with a checklist that can be completed item by item. Of course, you can talk about any other topics you may feel are relevant, but some sort of standardized process must be developed. We need to make sure that all of our clients are being educated on all of these specific topics in the same way, every time.

Phase two of turning leads into clients consists of information gathering. We absolutely need to have a clear, standardized questionnaire for all new clients to complete. The information-gathering phase should take one to two hours and is often combined with the education phase. We may have a meeting for a couple of hours with clients, where we are conducting the education phase and information gathering at the same time. In the information-gathering phase, we are trying to get a good viewpoint on or get good clarity on three primary areas of a client's world.

Number one is their current picture. What are they currently doing? What do they currently have, where are they currently invested? What kind of insurance risk management do they have in place? What's going on with their retirement at their job? All of these areas are important to delve into when we are in the information-gathering phase and trying to develop their current picture.

The second area we are trying to figure out is where they want to go. What are their goals and objectives? We first try to determine where they are, and then we try to determine where they want to go. When do they want to retire? How much do they need at retirement? What about college funds? Are they looking to pay off houses or are they going to sell houses? Are they going to move somewhere else? All of this needs to be considered and discussed in the second area of the information-gathering phase.

The third part of the information-gathering phase is determining their internal makeup. We are trying to find out how they view risk, how they view money, and what importance taxes hold in their overall financial plan. All three areas are critical components for behavioral coaching and dealing with the emotional side of their financial plan.

Phase three of turning leads into clients is analysis and plan creation. This happens on our own; we're actually not with the clients at this point. We're now doing our "financial planning job." We're now trying to see their weak points. What do we need to create? What do we need to change? What do we need to update? What do we want to have new? What do we want to get rid of? This is all key to plan creation. In this phase, it is important to use checklists, as it is easy to overlook an area because we're focused on so many different things. Checklists are absolutely critical during the plan analysis and creation phase.

Phase four consists of the presentation of the plan and the completion of paperwork. Traditional selling may come into place in this phase. I would say that, during all these phases, you're in selling mode. A book I would highly recommend in analyzing this specific phase and turning leads into clients is called *The SPIN Selling Fieldbook* by Neil Rackham.[23] "SPIN" isn't meant as a derogatory term here at all— it is simply an acronym for the four different types of questions that we ask. The book looks at the types of questions that we ask during the selling process or during the relationship management process when we are dealing with clients. Make sure to read the field book, not the actual book. The field book is much more practical and useful for advisors and sales professionals.

Phase five is the delivery and implementation. In phase three, we decide what we're actually going to do and the process going forward, and in phase four they are agreeing to the plan. In phase five, we are delivering the final plan documents, which often include new policies. Often, this particular phase is overlooked in the relationship management of clients. However, this is an important opportunity to reiterate some of the education points that we've discussed, along with some of the client's goals and objectives that we've covered together. We can actually tie all that back into what they're now receiving. A lot of savvy advisors use this as another marketing tool. They have wonderful binders personalized for their clients with their financial plans, all their documents, and everything in one place. Often, they provide two copies so clients can have one in a safe deposit box and one in their

---

23 Neil Rackham, *The Spin Selling Fieldbook* (New York, NY: McGraw-Hill, 1996).

office or their home. This is just another way to wow a client and be that purple cow.

The final phase of this process is phase six, which is turning clients into raving fans, which we'll cover in our next chapter.

Johnny says, "Now it makes sense to break the selling process into specific phases. One of the parts I missed, at least to the level that you're discussing, is the education part. I would educate prospects in relation to their specific situation and the solution I was proposing. I would only educate on a specific proposal for that client, as opposed to starting with education before I even began gathering information from them."

Sally replies, "You're not alone there. The entire industry made a shift toward broader education about twenty years ago. We've moved away from pitching products and trying to close clients to providing advice, diagnosing problems, and delivering solutions similar to the doctor/patient relationship. The problem is that clients want and need more."

She continues, "What has been found is that clients who are educated on the why's are much more inclined to stick with the plan during times of market, personal, or emotional stress. If they're educated only on their specific plan, without all of the why's behind it, then during times of stress they are likely to abandon the plan. Volatility and how we prepare for volatility is one of those critical education points that we must cover. We know that client's will experience volatility at some point and we know that many clients make poor emotional decisions during volatile times. Therefore, we must cover this area in advance so clients will know that there is a plan to deal with the inevitable volatility. Similarly we must educate on things like the S&P 500 and what it is and what is not, because they're going to hear a lot about the S&P in the news and they need to know how it applies or doesn't apply to their investments or their solutions."

Johnny says, "That makes total sense, and I can see the benefits of this. It's just a change from what I've been doing."

Sally interjects, "Remember the definition of insanity as doing the same thing over and over and expecting different results? It's time to do something different to get those different results."

> ## Exercise for the Reader:
>
> Write down what *you* think needs to be done to turn a lead into a client. While this chapter has provided one possible blueprint, you need to develop a system that fits your objectives, personality, and practice focus. List the specific steps that you need to take so as to convert your leads into clients.

CHAPTER 9:

Turning Clients into Raging Fans

Johnny says, "This is great stuff, Sally. I think I'm ready to get going on building a scalable business."

Sally says, "Actually, you aren't yet. At this point, you have a good financial practice, but now you need to transform your practice into a sustainable business. See, once you have clients, you need one more system in place designed to turn your clients into raving fans."

Johnny says, "Well, how do I do that?"

"You have to address seven critical areas to create raving fans," Sally says. "The two other essential components in turning clients from just ordinary clients to raving fans are loyalty and customer centricity. Let me tell you more about both of those."

Turning clients into raving fans is where we start to solidify our business for the long term. Everything the previous chapters covered was about laying the groundwork for our business, creating systems for our business, how we get prospects, and how we turn a prospect into a client. Now, we're solidifying our business for the long term, where we are turning our clients into not just fans, but raving fans.

The key to developing raving fans is all about loyalty. Loyalty is the key to a successful, growing, and sustainable business in any industry.

Five different books have affected me personally when it comes to turning clients into raving fans, and I'll touch upon each of these books in this chapter. One tremendous book called *The Ultimate Question 2.0*[24] delves into case study after case study of various businesses throughout all industries, from rental cars to financial services and everything in between. The essence is that loyalty is all about shutting your back door. You can have the best systems in the world to get people through your front door—getting new clients and getting new prospects—but if you lose existing clients at the same rate that you gain them, you're going nowhere. So, it's absolutely critical for you to create systems, and a process, to ensure that your back door is shut. It's all about developing loyalty, and the key to developing loyalty is creating raving fans. I would highly recommend reading through *The Ultimate Question 2.0* to gain a solid grasp for how loyalty is the key driver to creating raving fans.

As we look at developing raving fans, we can look to the Investor Dashboard Study, which shows the three top reasons for a client to be satisfied with their financial advisor are reputation and trust, relationship, and service.[25] All of these are interaction issues. You can't develop a good reputation and trust with your client if you don't have good service, you don't have good interactions, and you don't have good systems. Clients won't feel comfortable with you. You can't develop a relationship if you don't spend time getting to know clients below the surface. You need to get to know clients as people, as family members, and know what their roles are in life.

Obviously, service is a huge aspect in building loyalty. Without it, you can't develop loyal fans. You can't create raving fans unless you have a high level of service. These three important components in developing client satisfaction with your clients all focus on the quality

---

24 Frederick F. Reichheld and Rob Markey, *The Ultimate Question 2.0: How Net Promoter Companies Thrive in a Customer-Driven World*, Rev. and expanded ed. (Boston, MA: Harvard Business Press, 2011).

25 CEG_Worldwide, "Investor Dashboard: An in-Depth Look at Investor Behavior Trends," 11.

of your interactions with your clients. Once you can create satisfaction with your clients, then you are well on your way to developing raving fans and closing your back door.

The WOW Factor

Let's talk about WOW. WOW is about the customer experience that you're creating for your clients. There are two great books that I highly recommend that focus on this area specifically. One of them is by Jeffrey Gitomer, called *Customer Satisfaction Is Worthless; Customer Loyalty Is Priceless*.[26] The other one is called *Raving Fans,*[27] by Ken Blanchard. You may have noticed I used his term in the title of this chapter. Both of these books are tremendous books on the subject of developing raving fans and creating WOW!

You may be familiar with Ken Blanchard's style of writing from *The One-Minute Manager* and *The One-Minute Salesperson*. He makes his points through storytelling, provides a quick read, and really gets across the idea of what raving fans are. Mere fans aren't what we want. We want raving fans.

Jeffrey Gitomer's book goes into specific details on practical ways that you can develop loyalty, and how you can develop raving fans. These two tremendous books should be in the library of everyone who wants to build a successful business and develop raving fans.

In order to WOW your clients, a financial advisor must address seven critical areas. The first is their interactions. They need to have WOW systems in all of their interactions with their clients. That means they need to be friendly. They need to be professional. They need to be competent. They need to be concerned. They need to be thorough. And

---

[26] Jeffrey H. Gitomer, *Customer Satisfaction Is Worthless, Customer Loyalty Is Priceless: How to Make Customers Love You, Keep Them Coming Back and Tell Everyone They Know* (Austin, TX: Bard Press, 1998).

[27] Kenneth H. Blanchard and Sheldon M. Bowles, *Raving Fans: A Revolutionary Approach to Customer Service*, 1st ed. (New York, NY: Morrow, 1993).

all of it needs to look good. You can do all of those things, but if you're not friendly, it is not going to work. You can do all those things, but if all your written communications look terrible, if they contain misspellings or simply don't look professional, you're not going to win any fans. You can do all of those things, but if a client doesn't feel that you're concerned and empathetic to their situation, then none of it matters. You've got to be good at all six of those areas in all of your interactions with your clients—that includes your Facebook page, your website, your brochures, your office, your office manager, and your assistants. All of your touchpoints with your clients must have all six of those areas addressed.

Critical area number two is responsiveness. A surefire way to lose clients, and to generate the opposite of raving fans, is not to be responsive. Remember, the number one reason that clients switch advisors is that their service level drops. Clients indicate, in survey after survey, that three areas are important to them. The number one reason that they feel service drops, and that they are going to switch their advisor, is because of that advisor not returning calls in a timely fashion.

The number two reason is that the advisor is not proactive in contacting them, and the third top 5 reason clients fire their advisor is an advisor not returning emails in a timely manner. Breaking down this further, we know that one in four clients want a return call within two hours, and half want a return call the same day. But just to be sure, if you don't want to annoy one out of four clients, you've got to return calls within two hours. So, responsiveness is absolutely a critical component to building loyal, raving fans.

Number three is proactive communications. That means being proactive with emails, phone calls, newsletters, and regular meetings. It is important not to assume everybody wants to be communicated proactively with in the same manner. It is also very important during the onboarding process with a new client that you determine how often this client wants to be communicated with. Whatever they say, you should do it a little bit more. So, if they say, "If you call me twice a year, that's great," I call them four times a year.

Additionally, not everyone wants to be communicated with in the same manner. You may love to be communicated with by email. Someone else may love to be communicated with via phone calls, and another person would rather be communicated with directly, one-on-one, face to face. Therefore, you need to understand the frequency and the method the client would like to be communicated with, and do more than that to generate the WOW factor.

The fourth step in developing raving fans is life integration. That means your products and services must become an integral part of that individual's current and future life. You cannot just look at an individual transaction with your clients then move on. You need to go much, much deeper with your clients and look at how your products can touch various areas of their life on an ongoing basis.

With regard to life integration, it is not just your products that need to be integrated, but you also need to have in-depth intelligence on that particular client. There's a fantastic, old-school tool called the Mackay 66 Customer Profile which is in Harvey Mackay's book, *Swim with the Sharks without Being Eaten Alive*.[28]

The author, Harvey Mackay, says that if you want to create a moat around your clients to protect them from the competition, it is all about using their personal information to build that wall. Who are they? What are their interests? What schools did they go to? What sports teams do they follow? What are their hobbies? What are their kids' hobbies? What are their spouse's hobbies? What are their favorite vacation spots? What kind of restaurants do they go to? What is their favorite restaurant? What's their favorite wine? Do they even drink wine? Are they a beer person? Are they a teetotaler? All of those personal data points can be

---

28 Harvey Mackay, *Swim with the Sharks without Being Eaten Alive: Outsell, Outmanage, Outmotivate, Ad Outnegotiate Your Competition*, 1st ed. (New York, NY: Morrow, 1988).

found in profilers such as the Mackay 66, which is a great tool to begin with as you're developing a deeper relationship with your clients.

The fifth area in WOWing your clients is with social media. First, I'd like to begin with the idea that the best use of social media is not necessarily as a medium for posting information or presenting content. I want you to start thinking about social media as an intelligence-gathering tool. If I'm following my client on social media, and I see they just got a new puppy, I might then send this client a puppy welcome kit. They never told me they were getting a puppy, but if their financial advisor sends them a puppy welcome kit, they're going to be WOWed, which is exactly what we are striving for. This is how we WOW them with the information we glean from social media. Again, we do not want to think about social media solely as a way for us to provide information about us, which of course we can and should do, but we also need to think about the more important use of social media as an intelligence-gathering medium for our clients. We can see life events going on if we're using things like Facebook or Instagram or business events if we use platforms like LinkedIn. I want you think about social media as an intelligence-gathering tool, as opposed to an information presentation tool only.

The next step is what I call the above and beyond. Always think about how to do things above and beyond what your client expectations are. This is where we want to always under-promise and over-deliver. A perfect example of this is what I mentioned in the frequency of contact that the client requests. They say that they want to be contacted twice a year, but you should contact them four times a year. Always look for, in all areas of your interactions, how can you go above and beyond, where the client's going to think, "WOW, they really care about me. WOW, they really value me as a client and as a person." The above-and-beyond factor is an absolute critical component to wowing and developing raving fans.

Another area is the practical application of a good customer relationship tool. What are you using to track all of this information? There is no possible way that you can WOW and develop raving fans if you're not using information to get a leg up on your competition, and there's no way you're going to remember all of that information, or have it in note cards, or have it in notebooks. A very good CRM system is absolutely critical, and the gold standard for financial advisors is Redtail. Redtail is a fantastic CRM system, but more importantly, it interacts with most of the tools that today's financial advisors are using, from financial planning software, to consolidation software, to reporting software. It is one tool that we see the vast majority of successful advisors using currently. These are the seven critical areas that a financial advisor needs to focus in on if they're going to WOW their clients and develop raving fans.

Now, the final area that's important when it comes to WOWing clients and developing raving fans, is understanding that you're not going to be able to WOW everybody if you're trying to do the same things with completely disparate types of clients. In other words, you've got to have customer centricity. There's a great book called *Customer Centricity*,[29] which describes the need to analyze your client base. If you have 500 clients, you're probably not going to be able to WOW all of them because you just have too many people. You don't have enough time to return calls in two hours, or scour their Facebook pages, or have someone scour their Facebook pages for you. You'd have too many people to keep track of. As a result, it's absolutely important for you to utilize a process like customer centricity to analyze your clients.

Customer Centricity

Customer centricity entails a couple of steps. One is to look at your entire customer database and rank them in several areas. First, what is their current financial picture? Obviously, we are in the financial advisory business—the better their financial picture is, the greater chance you have of gathering more assets and generating more revenue. So, you'll want to rank them one through five. What is their potential long-term

---

29 Peter Fader, *Customer Centricity* (Philadelphia, PA: Wharton School Press, 2011).

financial picture? I know of a financial advisor who specializes in medical students. What a great area to focus on. Their current financial picture may not look too rosy, but their future financial picture looks fantastic. Developing that loyalty early on is important for building his particular business, and he's following my suggestion in Chapter 7 of focusing on a specific population to serve.

Clients could have all the money in the world, but if the next factor isn't there, it's not good for your business and not good for your emotional health. That is, "What clients do I most enjoy working with?" I think a lot of financial advisors overlook this. Instead, they go after the big fish, but they don't look at, "Am I going to enjoy working with the big fish? Who do I specifically enjoy working with?"

The final question is, "What does my ideal client look like, and does this person fit that mold?" You need to know what your ideal client looks like and rank all your clients from one to five in these four areas.

Once you've done that, there are three core principles of customer centricity. The first is to focus on your best customers. Some customers, simply put, are more valuable than others, and other customers are, to put it mildly, an absolute drain on your resources and your patience. When you strategically focus your energy on your best clients, you'll reap tremendous rewards.

Number two—commit to identifying your best customers. You must have an ongoing process in place, which I gave you above, to continually rank your customers on the four different areas. You must have that ongoing process in place to discover your customer lifetime value. In addition to understanding the traits of these best customers, you'll also want to learn what matters most to them in order to meet and exceed their expectations.

The third key principle of customer centricity is a willingness to invest in your best customers. It is not nearly enough to identify who your best customers are. You also have to make a commitment to allocate a disproportionate amount of your resources to them. These clients will provide you with the best return on investment, so you must invest in them. Do things like reviewing their Facebook pages on a weekly, ongoing basis—this could be having an assistant conduct this research. You could hire someone part-time, or you could employ an intern. An intern from a local college is often an excellent choice to help run your social media programs. They typically are adept at navigating all of the various social media platforms. Additionally, they may have other creative ideas in this area, based on their usage or experiences. You can easily have all of your social media activities done in a few hours a week, and interns could be a cost-effective way of getting this done.

Johnny says to Sally, "I'm still having trouble with customer centricity. I'm not sure what I should be doing in that area."

She replies, "Think of customer centricity as simply a way for you to analyze your clients to determine specifically where you should be investing your time and resources. Check out that book, *Customer Centricity*, if you really want to roll up your sleeves in this particular area. You've got to get the loyalty piece right and you've got to get the customer centricity piece right as well. So, make sure you take the time, energy, and effort to really get those two critical components down in creating a system from turning your clients into raving fans."

Exercise for the Reader:

What are five things that you can do today to turn your clients into raving fans? List them. Are you sending written thank you notes, birthday cards, and special event cards? Are you following ALL of your clients on social media and picking a few things each week to follow up on with your client base? Cultivating customer loyalty is one of the most important aspects of creating a successful and self-perpetuating business.

CHAPTER 10

Outsourcing Specifics

Johnny says, "This is all awesome. Is there anything else I should know before going forward?"

Sally says, "There is, in fact. One of the key areas of outsourcing is who you are going to outsource your investment management function to. Do you realize that, in just this one specific area, there is a $1 million difference in revenue between those who outsource and those who don't over a ten-year period?"

Johnny says, "The problem is, my value proposition for my clients is that I'm managing the money. If I outsource that piece, what's my value proposition?"

"Actually, your job is managing the client relationship and managing the outsource partners who help your clients achieve their financial goals," Sally says. "That is your value proposition. You need to be sitting on the same side of the table as your client across from those you outsource to, including the investment managers. Remember, if you're managing their money, you're sitting across the table from them. If you don't like how the investment management is going, the only solution for your client is to fire you. If you're on the same side of the table as your client and the investment manager is on the other side, if something's going wrong on the investment management side, you have an option as a team to either fire or make a change in investment managers. You're much more aligned with your clients when you're outsourcing that specific function."

She continues, "Remember two things—you are either a good asset manager or a good asset gatherer. Very rarely can you be good at both, especially if you want to build a scalable business. You can't chase both of those rabbits because you'll catch none. You can't be a jack of all trades and master of none. You need to master the client relationship process. Master the process of outsourcing and building your business in a scalable way, not by mastering investment management. Let people who are focused on that full-time take care of that function."

"Remember how we talked about head trash?" she asks. "Head trash is the value proposition myth. That's your head trash, not your clients'. You may feel that is your value proposition, but to your clients, that is not your value to them. Your value to them is guiding them along their financial journey to whatever their end objective is. It is not managing their money. That is not their value proposition of you. It's purely your head trash."

Johnny says, "So, do I just choose the best-performing management managers for my clients?"

Sally says, "Actually no. There are ten key areas that you must use to evaluate the managers you're going to use. It's not just all about performance. There are ten specific keys that you must utilize in analyzing the investment management firms that you're going to choose for your clients' portfolios."

The Importance of Outsourcing

This chapter will give some specific suggestions for outsourcing. To reiterate why outsourcing is important, I want to emphasize some of the statistics that we went over earlier. Do-it-yourselfers spend 37 percent of their day, on average, on investment research and portfolio rebalancing. In other words, in a nine-hour day, they spend three to four hours of their day working in this one area. Among more than 200 workdays in the year, they spend somewhere between fifty and a hundred workdays on investment research and portfolio rebalancing, versus those who outsource and spend 2 percent of their time on investment research and rebalancing.

Correspondingly, turnkey investors spend 56 percent of their time on business building activities—this includes meeting new clients, marketing, and meeting existing clients—versus 30 percent for do-it-yourselfers. Put another way, do-it-yourselfers spend 86 percent less time on business building activities than turnkey advisors. The conclusion is that do-it-yourselfers raise on average, $7.2 million a year versus $14.5 million a year for outsourcers. Those who outsource in their business raise double the amount of assets and make a lot more money than those who are trying to do it themselves and are reluctant to outsource.

What, Specifically, Should You Outsource?

Now we come to the question of what specifically to outsource. The biggest area that most financial advisors should consider outsourcing is the investment management function of their business. Financial advisors basically come to a point in their career where they can either become asset managers, so they get really good at managing money, or they become asset gatherers, where they're really good at managing relationships. All the statistics show that those who focus on the relationship management side, or the asset gathering side, make more money, have more time, and are more successful than those who try to do it all themselves.

Consequently, if we say that asset management is one of the biggest areas that we should be outsourcing, how do we do it and whom do we outsource it to? There are ten key areas that financial advisors should analyze and consider when they're looking at outsourcing their investment management to a partner or partners. Number one is that the investment manager needs to have a great story that the advisor can tell when it comes to the investment management thesis, idea, process, and company. What is that story? Is there a story? You can't just say, "Hey Client, we have a great product, and it works well," if there's no good story behind it. Stories are what capture people's imagination and having a good one is what's going to drive people to actually say, "Yes! I believe in that story."

First, you have to have a great story. Second, it has to work. You can't have a great story if you have something that doesn't work. When we say it has to work, that means there has to be some way of testing that it's legitimate. The ideal would be looking at a historical analysis through all market cycles. We would like to see how this particular investment product reacts in good markets and in bad markets. Lots of products work great in fantastic markets, but in down markets, they're horrible. Other products like CDs or U.S. treasuries work great in down markets, but don't work well in up markets, comparatively speaking. So, we need to look at and analyze all potential products historically, as far as how a product reacts in good markets and in bad markets. It has to work in all conditions.

Number three is an often-overlooked area for the advisor who is just starting to outsource their investment management function. This is that the product must be easy to explain and easy to understand. I've seen numerous products over the years that have a great story, and they work, but they're so complicated that no one can understand them. I can't explain them, my clients can't understand them, and therefore, my clients aren't going to stick with them. There's an old adage in sales that confused minds don't buy. With some products, it takes a Ph.D. in mathematics to even get an inkling of what they're trying to do. This is probably not going to be a product that you want to lean on as one of your core investment management outsourcing partners.

Number four, your product has got to be scalable. It doesn't do you any good, when you're trying to create a large and growing financial advisory practice, if your investment management partners can't grow with you. You can't just have an investment product whose premise is that they are looking for a specific inefficiency in the markets, but once they grow to a certain size, that inefficiency will no longer exist. You must have an investment management partner that is scalable and can grow with you.

Number five: Does this strategy play well with others? In other words, you want a strategy that fits in with other strategies. You really don't want to have a catch-all strategy, where there's just one thing that you're doing and that's it. Typically speaking, you want to have several investment management partners, or several investment product partners, that all fit and work well together. You may have some products that work better in up markets and some that work better in down markets, but they all work well together. You want non-correlated building blocks, as you're creating your investment management partnerships.

Number six—you want low cost. This doesn't mean that you want the cheapest solution, but you definitely want to have a lower-cost, higher-value solution. With a higher cost solution, you must either charge less, resulting in a decrease in your revenues and your profits, or charge more, and your client's performance suffers. Consequently, you want to make sure that you look at low-cost providers. Again, don't go with the cheapest or the lowest cost; instead, you're looking for a combination of low cost and high value.

Number seven is that your investment manager's process must be transparent. We do not want products that are shrouded in proprietary formulas, black boxes, or a cloud of secrecy. We MUST know the rules going in, and we must be able to explain the rules simply to our clients. This is very important, as the financial advisor needs to be able to manage their clients' expectations. If I do not know the rules, or if the product is cloaked in secrecy, I have no way of managing their expectations.

I really have no idea what is going to happen at any given time. Therefore, the solution partners that you choose must be transparent.

Number eight, it must be flexible. In other words, as I said earlier, we want products that work in good times and in bad times, and we want flexibility within that product lineup. We would rather work with a product partner that has multiple ways of combining their core building blocks to create different solutions for different demographics and different clients. In other words, we prefer not to work with a provider who has one product that does one thing all the time. We'd instead look for a partner who has several different building block core products that can be blended to create different outcomes and different solutions for different types of clients. If we are using different investment management partners who do only one thing, it just broadens the range of people we have to talk to and stories we must learn. In this case, we'd have twenty different investment partners versus three or four. You can see how that defeats the purpose of outsourcing, which is to save you time.

Number nine is that our investment management partner must have support available, and I don't mean monetary support. What we do want them to provide is intellectual capital. We want them to provide smarts. We want them to provide information and data that makes us, the financial advisors, look smarter, and quite frankly, more valuable to our clients. That's what's important. We want to ensure they have support available; again, not necessarily monetary support, but intellectual capital specifically.

The tenth and final thing is, again, one of those areas that we feel is often overlooked, and that's a mechanical process. We want to make sure that the product and the product providers that we lean on as our investment management outsource solutions are not based around emotional decision-making. The only way that we can ensure that is if we eliminate emotional decision-making and instead implement mechanical investment processes. We're looking for investment management processes that are mechanical and formulaic in nature. We know that emotional decision-making can, and will, affect the portfolio manager's decisions. We want to eliminate that completely. Studies show that mechanical, non-emotional decision-making beats out emotional, non-mechanical processes the majority of the time.

Additionally, non-mechanical, non-rules-based portfolio management gives a randomness to the returns and results that we cannot account for. As an example, let's say a portfolio manager was out sick for a day or two, so they weren't paying attention as they normally do. Let's also imagine that they didn't make a couple of trades they normally would have made, and because they didn't make those trades, it worked out for the positive, and thus their performance was enhanced by a completely random variable. How many different decisions were affected during the course of a year by random variables? We have no idea. One advisor once told me that they would much rather analyze a back-tested, mechanical, rules-based investment process than use the actual track record of a non-mechanical, non-rules-based portfolio manager. It is easy to see how the rules worked out, but we have ZERO way to account for the random variables that could be impacting the non-mechanical portfolio. We want to make sure that there is some sort of mechanical process that avoids variances caused by emotions and random events. We want to steer clear of this and eliminate it as much as possible with our investment management partners.

Another very important outsourced item is a technology outsource solution. You must have a strong CRM system. This is absolutely critical. I consider a CRM system as basically outsourcing somebody's memory into a computer. We don't need someone who's going to keep track of all the data among all of our clients because the CRM system is going to do it for us. The CRM system is going to create reminders. The CRM system can create automatic tasks. The CRM system is designed to keep a financial advisor's business on track and informed. While a CRM system is a great intelligence tool that we can use to keep track of all the information and data points on our clients, it is so much more because it can also automate tasks, it can create reminders, and it can generate numerous reports that give us a window into our business. A solid CRM system is absolutely essential for the scalable advisor.

Redtail is the most commonly used CRM within the financial advisory field. It is already designed for financial advisors with built in compatibility and has most of the commonly used tools in the financial advisor's arsenal.

Marketing is another area that can be outsourced. This is where we can outsource outbound phone calls, electronic marketing, seminar development organization, and website design. Many firms out there are turnkey financial advisory outsource solutions. Two that come to mind right now are White Glove and Snappy Kraken. Those firms provide numerous outsourced marketing solutions, specifically for the financial advisory community.

Compliance is one area that we feel MUST be outsourced. Many advisors are with broker dealers, for the simple reason that broker dealers provide that outsourced compliance solution. The broker dealer is taking care of it—the broker dealer is generating the systems, the filing processes that we all need to follow, and even doing inspections of our offices or other financial advisors' offices, to ensure compliance with all of the current regulatory reforms, regulatory bulletins, notices, new rules, and new laws. What broker dealers provide in this area alone is invaluable. Many advisors have a somewhat adversarial role with their compliance departments, but they are there for all of our protection, and they unfortunately have the thankless task of telling us "no." Learn to work with your compliance department, and try to begin to view things from their point of view; it will make your life and theirs a little bit easier…hopefully.

However, many advisors are deciding to break away from broker dealers, and they now have the quandary of handling their compliance function within their own stand-alone firm. Several firms specialize in outsource compliance solutions; I highly recommend that, if an advisor is breaking away to be a standalone RIA, they consider seriously outsourcing this function. This is not a function to play with. You don't want to mess up in the compliance area because this is an area that can put you out of business. This is critically important for advisors to outsource.

Another area is research. Advisors can outsource their research function for keeping up to date on the markets and the economy in general. Advisors should definitely not be doing this research themselves. Numerous services provide data on economics, financial markets, specific investment solutions, and taxes. Outsourcing your research solution means that you don't have to keep on top of all the different happenings, changes, and updates in the regulatory, the economic, and the financial markets, but you can still look like a genius to your clients in those areas. One suggestion is to try and get this research provided to you for free from your investment management partners.

A Solution for Miscellaneous Tasks

The final thing that I want to say about outsourcing is that I want to recommend a specific outsource solution that can be used for many areas in an advisor's business. This is the solution we discussed previously, Upwork. Upwork.com is a community of freelancers around the world. Tens of thousands of freelancers on Upwork can do a myriad of tasks for a very low cost. Some examples are researching names, gathering email addresses, creating logos, updating websites, creating email campaigns, writing brochures, doing the graphics for brochures, creating new apps, updating spreadsheets, or whatever mundane and menial tasks you may need done. Even more complex tasks such as programming a website can be accomplished on Upwork for a low cost and in a timely fashion. I highly recommend that advisors get familiar with Upwork and start thinking about what areas in their business can they outsource to solutions such as these.

Spend some time exploring Upwork, as you will find freelancers who can do just about everything. I have had over four different freelancers working on various projects at one time. I have really relied on it for the creative side of my business. They have created videos, edited videos, provided voice overs, redesigned PowerPoint presentations, created logos, and so on. One thing that I have done is to hire two freelancers for a single job. This allows me to see two different versions of an idea (e.g., a presentation) and decide which one is best for what I am looking to accomplish. The cost is so low that it is easy to complete projects in this fashion.

Another example where I have used Upwork frequently is in the creation of fillable forms. I was in a meeting with an advisor, who was trying to create a fillable questionnaire for his clients. I was able to email an Upwork freelancer whom I had used previously and get the form created and polished in less than fifteen minutes. To sum up, I cannot recommend Upwork highly enough to outsource miscellaneous tasks that you might not otherwise consider outsourcing.

Johnny says, "Okay, I get it. Outsourcing is the key to building a scalable business, and the most important area that I must outsource is the investment management function, and there are ten key areas I must take a look at when choosing an investment management partner."

Sally says, "I think you've got it."

> **Exercise for the Reader:**
>
> Go back to the exercise from Chapter 5, and rethink what you have written. Can you add anything else? Now, spend a little bit of time writing out how much of your time, that nonrenewable resource, that you are spending on each of these areas. Start researching your various outsourcing options using some of the ideas provided in this chapter.

Conclusion

Johnny says, "I am sold. It all makes total sense."

Sally says, "I'm glad you're sold, but that's not enough. You now have the hardest part, which is is actually doing it. I failed in the beginning when I first started creating my scalable business. It's not easy."

"I fully understand that it's not easy," Johnny says, "but I've got a jumpstart with you helping me in creating everything I need to be successful. I know the concept of time as a nonrenewable resource. I know how to get off the income and sales funnel roller coaster. I know that working on my business is the most important thing that I invest my time in, as opposed to spending time just working in my business. I understand I have to clear my mind of the head trash or the misconceptions because that's what is going to prevent me from changing and doing new things."

He continues, "I know the key to a scalable business is outsourcing. I know that I've got to create systems for my entire business, and the key to systems is checklists. I've got to create three primary systems—generating leads, how to turn those leads into clients, and how to turn those clients into raving fans. Finally, I have some specifics on how to pick one of my most critical outsourcing partners, my investment managers."

Sally says, "You definitely have it all, but that is the easy part. The understanding of why and what to do is easy. The hard part is the actual doing and, sticking to the doing. Planning and execution equals success. You cannot have one without the other."

The only way that we can go about creating a viable, growing, successful, large business and also have a life at the same time is through scalability. You must work on your business, not just in your business. We discussed key areas with regards to this throughout the book. In the early chapters, we discussed how your business can eventually run you instead of you running your business. In the middle chapters, we discussed how to take back your life and create a scalable business through outsourcing and creating systems. In the final chapters, we went through some specific solutions you need to develop and create to have a thriivng, scalable business.

You have the tools in place; all you need now is to do it. Your choice is either to do it all yourself, which entails having less time to grow your business, having less time with your family, gathering fewer assets, and making less money, or you can build a scalable business. By outsourcing and creating systems, you will have more time to build your business, more time for family, more time to do the things you want, and more time to make more money. And there are not many trade-offs like that, right? You can have more time, more things you want, more money, and a freer life, or make less money, spend more time, and have a business that controls your life. It's really a "duh" choice.

But it's not going to be easy. This isn't something that's going to happen overnight. It's not something that's going to happen without effort. What we have seen is that you can either try to go it alone and do it all yourself or you can get someone to help you, to coach you along the way, to be your partner in your success. That's where we've seen advisors have the greatest degree of success. A perfect example of this is an advisor that we worked with who built up about $50 million in assets under management over roughly a ten-year period. He rented a small office. He was trying to do most things by himself. He was trying to be all things to all people, and his thought was that no one could do his business like he could do his business. He was trying to do everything for himself by himself. He was trying to be all things to all people with all his different clients; he had no time for his family. He had no time for his outside interests.

Then he got a coach who really helped him analyze his business. This coach helped this advisor create systems and also helped him narrow his focus. In helping him create systems, the coach asked: What can he outsource? What does he not need to be doing in his office? What does he not need to be doing that's on his desk that he can ship to somebody else's desk or outsource?

Probably just as important, the coach helped focusing his business on a niche market. He went through a process of dumping clients who didn't fit his target. This even included some multimillionaire clients whom a lot of people think would be ideal targets, but they didn't fit his ideal client profile and he eventually dumped these clients.

Now, a few years later, this advisor actually has a smaller office. He has fewer employees than he did. He has less overhead. He outsources obsessively, and he has over triple the assets than he did before this process. It took this advisor ten years to get to $50 million, and it took him about three or four years to go to $150 million with fewer people and less overhead.

As you can imagine, his profit margin is soaring through the roof. He's making a ton of money and, more importantly he has more time with his family. He's able to travel with his family internationally. Plus, he is now able to spend more time on his own interests outside of the business. His story is the definition of a tremendous business and a tremendous life.

Additionally, he was managing most of his own portfolios when he had the $50 million book of business. He manages none of his portfolios today. Now, he focuses on managing his client relationships. When I talk to that advisor, he says it's amazing how he has much deeper relationships. Even though he has more clients now than he had back then, he has deeper relationships and spends more time with each one than he did back when he had only a third of his current clients and a third of the assets. He has much greater life satisfaction now that he's spending more quality time developing deeper relationships, having more time with his family, having more time for outside interests, and making more money, all because of building a scalable business. In his case, hiring a partner who was a coach was a key step. Now he has a fully scalable business making well north of seven figures net, all while freed up from the burdens and time demands he had when he was a do-it-yourselfer.

He couldn't have done all that heavy lifting, especially in the early stage, without someone guiding him, coaching him, supporting him, and providing a sounding board for his challenges and ideas. A lot of financial advisors seem to be on an island by themselves. They have office support, but someone who has the same business interest and alignment that the advisor is trying to develop is a rarity. As a result, getting that kind of partner in success is very important. It's not a requirement, but it sure can make your life a lot easier when trying to build a scalable business.

A scalable business will make it much easier for you to have a tremendous business and a tremendous life. There are key steps to getting, building, and developing a successful scalable business. And more than likely, you're going to have an easier go of it if you have a partner in that journey in going from being a do-it-yourselfer to a having fully scalable enterprise.

Johnny asks Sally, "But how did you do it, and how did you execute?"

"I had a coach," Sally says, "to help me along the way. There wasn't a book to guide me along. I wish there had been. Fortunately, now there is, but you still may need help along the way, which is why I recommend either a coach or a study group of like-minded advisors. With either of these options, you have the support that you're going to need to stick to your journey in building a sustainable, scalable business."

BONUS CHAPTER

Scalable Essentials

Ten Essential Books for the Scalable Library

The E-Myth: Why Most Businesses Don't Work and What to Do About It, by Michael E. Gerber. Cambridge, MA: Ballinger Pub., 1986.

Swim with the Sharks without Being Eaten Alive: Outsell, Outmanage, Outmotivate, And Outnegotiate Your Competition, by Harvey Mackay. 1st ed. New York, NY: Morrow, 1988.

The Checklist Manifesto: How to Get Things Right, by Atul Gawande. 1st ed. New York, NY: Metropolitan Books, 2010.

Raving Fans: A Revolutionary Approach to Customer Service by Kenneth H. Blanchard and Sheldon M. Bowles. 1st ed. New York, NY: Morrow, 1993.

Customer Satisfaction Is Worthless, Customer Loyalty Is Priceless: How to Make Customers Love You, Keep Them Coming Back and Tell Everyone They Know by Jeffrey H. Gitomer. Austin, TX: Bard Press, 1998.

The Ultimate Question 2.0: How Net Promoter Companies Thrive in a Customer-Driven World, by Frederick F. Reichheld and Rob Markey. Revised. and expanded ed. Boston, MA: Harvard Business Press, 2011.

The Purple Cow: Transform Your Business by Being Remarkable by Seth Godin. New York, NY: Portfolio, 2009.

Customer Centricity by Peter Fader. Philadelphia, PA: Wharton School Press, 2011.

The SPIN Selling Fieldbook, by Neil Rackham. New York, NY: McGraw-Hill, 1996.

Expecting Referrals: The Resurrection of a Lost Art, by Scott A. Kramnick. Fredericksburg, VA: Associates Publishing, 1993.

Three Steps to Getting Control of Your Time

1. Track your time in 15-minute increments for at least one week. (Two is preferred).
2. Review the usage of your time and look at your time wasters. Strive to eliminate at least 25 percent of your activities as time wasters.
3. Plan your time usage in blocks of time of at least one-hour blocks (two-hour blocks are better) doing similar tasks. For example, two hours of prospecting calls, one hour of social media marketing, or two hours of client review preparation. The key is, during these blocks, to do nothing except those tasks assigned to that particular block of time.

The Five Reasons Someone Will Listen to You

Make sure that all of your messaging takes these five reasons into account:

1. Need
2. Greed

3. Fear
4. Friendship
5. Curiosity

The Six Steps to Turn Prospects into Clients

1. Education on Key Concepts
2. Information Gathering
3. Information Analysis and Plan Creation
4. Presentation of Plan and Completion of Paperwork
5. Delivery and Implementation
6. Turn the Clients into Raving Fans

The Seven Topics All Prospects Must Be Educated on Before They Become Your Client

1. The importance of Diversification
2. What the S&P 500 is and what is it not
3. Asset Allocation and Modern Portfolio Theory
4. What is systematic risk?
5. The mathematic impact of losses on portfolio results
6. Risk Management both for portfolios and life events
7. Emotions and how they can get us in trouble

The Seven Critical Areas of WOW: How to Turn Clients into Raving Fans

1. All interactions must be WOW—Six Keys
   a. Friendly
   b. Professional
   c. Competent
   d. Concerned (empathetic)
   e. Thorough
   f. Looking good
2. Responsiveness—are you returning calls and emails in a timely fashion? Two hours or less is preferred.
3. Proactively Communicating with Clients—do you know how often and how each client wants to be communicated with?
4. Life Integration—your services and products must be integrated into their life. A big key here is information about your client. Think of the Mackay 66.
5. Social Media used as an information gathering tool
6. Above and beyond! Always over deliver and under promise. What can you do that your client wouldn't expect?
7. The customer Relationship Management (CRM) System is a MUST, and you MUST use it!

Ten Key Traits of an Investment Management Partner

1. They must have a great story that makes sense.
2. It has to work through all market conditions in both good and bad markets.

3. It must be easy to explain and easy to understand.

4. The product must be scalable.

5. The product works well with other products. It complements other products well—for instance, a tactical manager paired with a strategic manager is often a good complimentary combination.

6. Is it low cost? Not the cheapest, but low cost with high value is what we should be striving for.

7. Is it transparent or is it shrouded in proprietary formulas and black boxes or a process so confusing that it is virtually impossible to decipher?

8. Flexibility: Can you use the investment management partners, product in a variety of ways for a variety of clients and a variety of risk profiles?

9. Does the investment manager have support available to advisor partners? This is not monetary support, but more along the line of intellectual support.

10. Is their process mechanical? Emotions can get the best of clients, advisors, AND portfolio managers. They are humans too, and studies have shown that the herd mentality is very strong in the investment management space. It is better to be wrong if we are all wrong than to stick to a strong investment thesis. Therefore, a mechanical, rules-based approach is preferred for your core investment management partners.

About the Author

Dan Baccarini has been in the financial services industry since 1993 when he started out as a financial advisor. He quickly became a producing manger overseeing a region of 20 advisors in the Midwest. Dan began working with asset managers in the late 90's helping them build their distribution efforts through broker dealers. This brought Dan into contact with thousands of financial advisors where he was able to observe what worked and what didn't work in building a successful advisory practice. Most recently he has helped build broker dealer distribution for Beacon Capital Management where he oversaw asset growth from about $250M to over $3B. Dan continues to meet with hundreds of advisors annually to keep up to date as to the best practices of the most successful financial advisors in the country. He is a CIMA®, has his MBA and has held the Series 7, 24, 63 and 65 licenses.

To learn more, please visit my website at:
www.ScalabilityForAdvisors.com

References

Anderson, John D., Brad Bueermann, and Raef Lee. "A Data-Backed Solution to Building a More Profitable Advisory Business." SEI, 2016.

Blanchard, Kenneth H., and Sheldon M. Bowles. *Raving Fans: A Revolutionary Approach to Customer Service.* 1st ed. New York, NY: Morrow, 1993.

CEG_Worldwide. "Investor Dashboard: An in-Depth Look at Investor Behavior Trends." Vanguard, 2018.

Drucker, Peter F. *The Essential Drucker: The Best of Sixty Years of Peter Drucker's Essential Writings on Management.* 1st Collins Business Essentials ed. New York, NY: Collins Business Essentials, 2008.

Fader, Peter. *Customer Centricity.* Philadelphia, PA: Wharton School Press, 2011.

Furey, John, and Matt Cooper. "What Is Your Advisory Practice Really Worth?" *WealthManagement Magazine*, 2013.

Gawande, Atul. *The Checklist Manifesto: How to Get Things Right.* 1st ed. New York, NY: Metropolitan Books, 2010.

Gerber, Michael E. *The E-Myth: Why Most Businesses Don't Work and What to Do About It.* Cambridge, MA: Ballinger Pub., 1986.

Gitomer, Jeffrey H. *Customer Satisfaction Is Worthless, Customer Loyalty Is Priceless: How to Make Customers Love You, Keep Them Coming Back and Tell Everyone They Know.* Austin, TX: Bard Press, 1998.

Godin, Seth. *The Purple Cow: Transform Your Business by Being Remarkable.* New York, NY: Portfolio, 2009.

Heiman, Stephen E., Diane Sanchez, and Tad Tuleja. *The New Strategic Selling: The Unique Sales System Proven Successful by the World's Best Companies.* Warner Books ed. New York, NY: Warner Books, 1998.

Kramnick, Scott A. *Expecting Referrals: The Resurrection of a Lost Art.* Fredericksburg, VA: Associates Publishing, 1993.

Mackay, Harvey. *Swim with the Sharks without Being Eaten Alive: Outsell, Outmanage, Outmotivate, Ad Outnegotiate Your Competition.* 1st ed. New York, NY: Morrow, 1988.

Matrisian, Matt. "The True Value of Your Practice." *FA Magazine*, March 2, 2015 2015.

Rackham, Neil. *The Spin Selling Fieldbook.* New York, NY: McGraw-Hill, 1996.

Reichheld, Frederick F., and Rob Markey. *The Ultimate Question 2.0: How Net Promoter Companies Thrive in a Customer-Driven World.* Rev. and expanded ed. Boston, MA: Harvard Business Press, 2011.

Spectrem_Group. "The Affluent Investor: Insights and Opportunities for Advisors." 2016.

Made in the USA
Middletown, DE
10 February 2021